Is Torture
Ever Justified?

Is Torture
Ever Justified?

Other books in the At Issue series:

Alternatives to Prisons
Anorexia
Antidepressants
Anti-Semitism
Are Athletes Good Role Models?
Are Chain Stores Ruining America?
Are Privacy Rights Being Violated?
Attention Deficit/Hyperactivity Disorder
Biological and Chemical Weapons
Child Labor and Sweatshops
Child Sexual Abuse
Cosmetic Surgery
Creationism Versus Evolution
Do Children Have Rights?
Does Advertising Promote Substance Abuse?
Does the Internet Benefit Society?
Does the Internet Increase the Risk of Crime?
Does the United States Need a National Health Insurance
    Policy?
Drugs and Sports
The Ethics of Abortion
The Future of the Internet
How Can the Poor Be Helped?
How Should One Cope with Death?
How Should Society Address the Needs of the Elderly?
How Should the United States Treat Prisoners in the War on
    Terror?
Indian Gaming
Is American Culture in Decline?
Is Islam a Religion of War or Peace?
Is It Unpatriotic to Criticize One's Country?
Islam in America
Is Poverty a Serious Problem?
Is the Gap Between the Rich and Poor Growing?
Is There Life After Death?
Is the World Heading Toward an Energy Crisis?
Legalizing Drugs
Managing America's Forests
Nuclear and Toxic Waste
Protecting America's Borders
Religion and Education
Space Exploration
Teen Sex
What Are the Most Serious Threats to National Security?
What Causes Addiction?
Women in Islam

At ✳ Issue

Is Torture Ever Justified?

Tom Head, *Book Editor*

Bruce Glassman, *Vice President*
Bonnie Szumski, *Publisher*
Helen Cothran, *Managing Editor*

GREENHAVEN PRESS
An imprint of Thomson Gale, a part of The Thomson Corporation

THOMSON
™
GALE

Detroit • New York • San Francisco • San Diego • New Haven, Conn.
Waterville, Maine • London • Munich

For more information, contact
Greenhaven Press
27500 Drake Rd.
Farmington Hills, MI 48331-3535
Or you can visit our Internet site at http://www.gale.com

LIBRARY OF CONGRESS CATALOGING-IN-PUBLICATION DATA

Is torture ever justified? / Tom Head, book editor.
    p. cm. — (At issue)
  Includes bibliographical references and index.
  ISBN 0-7377-3109-5 (lib. : alk. paper) — ISBN 0-7377-3110-9 (pbk. : alk. paper)
    1. Torture. 2. Political prisoners—Abuse of. 3. Military interrogation—United States. 4. Terrorism—Investigation—United States. 5. Torture—Iraq. 6. Political prisoners—Abuse of—Iraq. 7. Iraq War, 2003—Prisoners and prisons, American. 8. Abu Ghraib prison. I. Head, Tom. II. At issue (San Diego, Calif.)
  HV8593.I75 2005
  364.6'7—dc22   2004059764

Contents

Page

Introduction   9

1. Torture Is Never Justified   12
   Kenneth Roth

2. Torture Is Sometimes Justified   16
   Henry Mark Holzer

3. Torture Should Be Legalized and Regulated   22
   Alan M. Dershowitz

4. The U.S. Military Need Not Obey the Geneva
   Conventions When Dealing with Suspected Terrorists   26
   John Yoo

5. The U.S. Military Should Always Obey the Geneva
   Conventions   31
   Lincoln Caplan

6. "Stress and Duress" Techniques Are Forms of Torture   35
   Tom Malinowski

7. "Stress and Duress" Techniques Are Legitimate Forms
   of Interrogation   39
   Mark Bowden

8. The Use of Torture Serves Current U.S. Foreign Policy
   Objectives   54
   Glen T. Martin

9. The Abu Ghraib Prisoner Abuse Qualifies as Torture   59
   The Medical Foundation for the Care of Victims of Torture

10. The Abu Ghraib Prisoner Abuse Does Not Qualify
    as Torture   65
    Ilana Freedman

11. The Abu Ghraib Prisoner Abuse Was Committed
    by a Few Disobedient Soldiers   69
    Tammy Bruce

12. The Abu Ghraib Prisoner Abuse Was Authorized by   74
    High-Ranking Government Officials
      Eric Boehlert

13. The U.S. News Media Overrated the Significance of   81
    the Abu Ghraib Prisoner Abuse
      Oliver North

Organizations to Contact   85

Bibliography   88

Index   90

Introduction

In June 1979 Jean Leon and an accomplice kidnapped Miami cab driver Louis Gachelin, held him at gunpoint, and demanded a seven-thousand-dollar ransom from his family. Police officers quickly captured Leon, but Gachelin was not with him. Concerned that Gachelin might be murdered once Leon's absence was noticed by his accomplice, seven police officers made a radical decision: To find out where Gachelin was being held, they beat the information out of Leon. The kidnapper caved in, and Gachelin was rescued. His life had arguably been saved by the use of torture.

Torture is the deliberate infliction of pain for pain's sake. It can be used to punish and intimidate or to gather information, and has been put to use to achieve these ends for the entire recorded history of human civilization. The Code of Hammurabi, dated 1750 B.C., threatens death by torture by means of fire, water, or impaling. Crucifixion, used to execute Jesus in A.D. 33, was a form of public torture routinely used to punish Jewish revolutionaries who opposed the Roman order. Even today, laws decreeing death by torture are frighteningly common in many parts of the world.

Most Americans would not advocate that their government should use torture as a means of punishment, a practice the Eighth Amendment (prohibiting "cruel and unusual punishment") specifically excludes. Rather, the current debate centers on situations very similar to the Gachelin case: situations involving torture as an interrogation technique in urgent cases of life and death. Such cases have historically been so rare that the question of justifiable torture has become more an issue of philosophy than an issue of public policy.

The attacks of September 11, 2001, however, rekindled the torture debate. Since the horrifying terrorist attacks on New York and Washington, D.C., every branch of U.S. law enforcement has focused primarily on how to prevent similar events from occurring in the future. One possible way to prevent terrorist attacks is to learn about plots before they are carried out. This, though, involves extracting information from terrorists who are extremely unlikely to volunteer information. In this case, some Americans have argued for using torture to get them to divulge information. Others have maintained that torture is never justified and cannot be supported under any circumstances.

Opponents of torture generally make two points: that torture is irredeemably inhumane, and that it does not really work very well. As one May 2004 editorial in the British newspaper the *Guardian* argues: "In real life, there are no simple ethical dilemmas. There are no ticking timebombs that need only a gouged eye or broken jaw to be uncovered. . . . Torture is more a sign of desperation, an admission that your side has no other resources left. . . . This is no moral slippery slope, this is a sheer drop into an immoral abyss."

Those who defend the use of torture argue that the imperative to save human lives should outweigh other concerns. Political commentator and former presidential candidate Patrick J. Buchanan argues that inflicting pain on suspected terrorists is the most moral choice, given the available options:

> If doctors can cut off limbs and open up hearts to save lives, and cops may shoot criminals to save lives, and the state may execute criminals, why cannot we commit a lesser evil . . . for a far greater good: preventing the murder of innocents? What will history say about people who . . . recoil in horror from painfully extracting the truth out of one mass murderer to stop the almost certain slaughter of their own people?

As the debate over torture continues, the U.S. government has experimented with interrogation techniques that can serve the same purpose as torture without violating U.S. or international law. These are known as "stress and duress" techniques, which consist of exposing prisoners to isolation, darkness, blindfolding, discomfort (such as being forced to stand in one position for four hours), forced nudity, and unpleasant food. These tactics are designed to demoralize prisoners so that they will provide information, and they have been met with much controversy over the legality and morality of their application.

Those in favor of using the intensified techniques argue that the information extracted from "stressed" prisoners might save hundreds of lives. As author Tammy Bruce puts it,

> I don't care if you put women's underwear on their heads, or frankly, even pull out a few fingernails of

those responsible for mass murder, to unmask their continuing plans for the genocide of civilized peoples. . . . It's called "torture lite," it works, and I'm all for whatever it takes to get information, and yes, to punish and annihilate terrorist leadership around the world.

On the other hand, those who oppose such techniques argue that they do in fact constitute forms of torture, and as such are prohibited by U.S. and international law. As Kenneth Roth, executive director of Human Rights Watch, explains:

None of these techniques is legal. Treaties ratified by the United States, including the Geneva Conventions and the U.N. Convention Against Torture, prohibit not only torture but also "cruel, inhuman or degrading treatment or punishment." . . . In other words, just as U.S. courts repeatedly have found it unconstitutional for interrogators in American police stations to use these third-degree methods, it is illegal under international law for U.S. interrogators . . . elsewhere to employ them.

The U.S. torture debate was revived by the threat of terrorism, and the outcome of the debate may depend on the existence of future terrorist attacks. If the September 11 attacks prove to be an aberration, Americans may look back and marvel on the fact that torture was seriously considered as an interrogation option. If attacks of similar magnitude do occur in the future, then many may continue to advocate torture as a means of preventing future tragedies.

1

Torture Is Never Justified

Kenneth Roth

Kenneth Roth is the executive director of Human Rights Watch, a nonprofit organization dedicated to defending human rights around the world.

International treaties ban torture not only because it is inhumane but also because it is ineffective. Prisoners who are tortured will say anything to have the torture stop; therefore, any information extracted from them is unreliable. Because some officials will always resort to coercion, many analysts recommend regulating torture. However, regulating the practice tacitly condones it and encourages more abuse of prisoners. Since the United States is a signatory to international treaties banning torture, it should not allow the torturing of prisoners in the war on terrorism.

The sexual humiliation of [Iraqi] prisoners [by U.S. soldiers] at Abu Ghraib prison [in Iraq] is so shocking that it risks overshadowing other U.S. interrogation practices that are also reprehensible. And unlike the sexual abuse, these other practices have been sanctioned by the highest levels of government and are probably more widespread.

The Abu Ghraib outrages are not simply the product of a small group of sick and misguided soldiers. They are the predictable result of the Bush administration's policy of permitting "stress and duress" interrogation techniques. The sexual abuse of prisoners, despicable as it is, is a logical consequence of a system put in place after [the terrorist attacks of] Sept. 11, 2001, to ratchet up the pain, discomfort and humiliation of prisoners under interrogation.

A Stress Matrix

The Defense Department has adopted a 72-point "matrix" of types of stress to which detainees can be subjected. These include stripping detainees naked, depriving them of sleep, subjecting them to bright lights or blaring noise, hooding them, exposing them to heat and cold, and binding them in uncomfortable positions. The more stressful techniques must be approved by senior commanders, but all are permitted. And nearly all are being used, according to testimony taken by [the human rights organization] Human Rights Watch from post–Sept. 11 detainees released from U.S. custody.

None of these techniques is legal. Treaties ratified by the United States, including the Geneva Conventions and the U.N. Convention Against Torture, prohibit not only torture but also "cruel, inhuman or degrading treatment or punishment." In ratifying the Convention Against Torture, the U.S. government interpreted this provision to prohibit the same practices as those proscribed by the U.S. Constitution. The Bush administration reiterated that understanding [in] June [2003].

In other words, just as U.S. courts repeatedly have found it unconstitutional for interrogators in American police stations to use these third-degree methods, it is illegal under international law for U.S. interrogators in Iraq, Afghanistan, Guantanamo Bay [Cuba, where terror suspects are held] or elsewhere to employ them. U.S. military manuals ban these "stress and duress" techniques, and federal law condemns them as war crimes. Yet the Bush administration has authorized them.

No Extraordinary Response Is Necessary

But doesn't the extraordinary threat of terrorism demand this extraordinary response? No. The prohibition of torture and cruel, inhuman, or degrading treatment or punishment is absolute and unconditional, in peace or in war. This dehumanizing practice is always wrong.

Moreover, resorting to abusive interrogation is counterproductive. People under torture will say anything, true or not. And whatever marginal advantage interrogators might gain by applying these techniques is vastly outweighed by the global disgust at American use of them. Coupled with anger at other lawless practices, such as the Bush administration's refusal to apply the Geneva Conventions to the Guantanamo detainees,[1] that revulsion has contributed to America's plummeting esteem. Allies are less willing to cooperate in combating terrorism, and terrorist recruiters must be having a field day.

> **//** *Treaties ratified by the United States . . . prohibit not only torture but also 'cruel, inhuman or degrading treatment or punishment.'* **//**

But can't torture at least be used on someone who might know of an imminent terrorist act? Not without opening the door to pervasive torture. The problem with this "ticking bomb" scenario is that it is infinitely elastic. Why stop with the terrorist suspect himself? Why not torture his neighbor or friend who might know something about an attack? And why stop with an imminent attack? Aren't the potential victims of possible future attacks just as worthy of protection by torture? The slope is very slippery.

Regulation Would Be Problematic

It has been argued that because some interrogators will inevitably resort to coercion, torture should be regulated. But by signaling that torture and mistreatment are sometimes justified, regulation ends up encouraging more Abu Ghraibs.

Government officials are also notoriously poor at regulating coercive interrogation techniques. For example, Israel's effort to regulate the application of "moderate physical pressure" led to deaths in custody and ultimately a decision by Israel's Supreme Court to outlaw it. Human Rights Watch and others have repeatedly reported abusive techniques on the part of U.S. interrogators, but the Bush administration did nothing to address

1. The author refers to the controversy over status of the detainees held at Guantanamo Bay, Cuba. The Bush administration argues that the detainees should be designated as "enemy combatants" because they fought for no particular country; this exempts them from the rights of prisoners of war protected by the Geneva Conventions.

them until the photographs of Abu Ghraib became public. Indeed, to this day, no one has been prosecuted for two deaths of detainees in U.S. custody in Afghanistan; medical examiners declared those deaths "homicides" a year and a half ago.

Maj. Gen. Geoffrey D. Miller announced last week [May 2004] that certain stress interrogation techniques will no longer be used in Iraq. That's a useful first step. President Bush should now ban all forms of "stress and duress" interrogation, in Iraq and elsewhere. Various noncoercive methods, from inducements to trickery, can still be used, as able interrogators have done for decades. And no one contends that detention centers should be country clubs. But the deliberate ratcheting up of pain, suffering and humiliation as an interrogation technique must be stopped. It is wrong itself, and it leads to further atrocities.

2

Torture Is Sometimes Justified

Henry Mark Holzer

Henry Mark Holzer is a law professor at Brooklyn Law School. He is author of eight books, including Sweet Land of Liberty? The Supreme Court and Individual Rights *(1982) and* Speaking Freely: The Case Against Speech Codes *(1994).*

It is likely that a clear majority of Americans would support torture in cases where it can prevent massive loss of life. The use of torture in such situations is not only morally permissible, but also morally necessary. A legal precedent for torture can be found in a Florida case where police officers threatened and physically abused a kidnapping suspect in an attempt to locate his victim, and were lauded in both state and federal court rulings. Most would consider this use of physical abuse acceptable because it saved the victim's life. If it is acceptable to use physical abuse and threats to save lives, then it should be acceptable to use nonlethal torture—particularly when dealing with a terrorist's "ticking bomb" scenario, where countless lives may be at risk.

[In 2002] we witnessed Chechen rebels [fighting to make Chechnya independent from Russia] taking over a Moscow theater, capturing hundreds of hostages, and threatening to kill them if the intruders' demands were not met. Let's assume the same thing happens in the United States, but with al-Qaeda terrorists. Assume further that we capture one of the terrorists who knows the plans of his comrades, but he won't talk. Should we

Henry Mark Holzer, "In Defense of Torture," *Front Page Magazine*, November 29, 2002. Copyright © 2002 by the Center for the Study of Popular Culture. Reproduced by permission.

use torture to force this crucial information out of him?

"Torture"—commonly defined as "the inflicting of severe pain to force information or confession"—comes principally in two varieties: physical (e.g., the "third degree") and psychological (e.g., sleep deprivation). The literature on torture is voluminous, most commentators concluding that torture is odious and unacceptable at *all* times and under *all* circumstances, especially in a democracy.

But is it?

The Ticking Time Bomb

Some of the commentators, in their analysis and discussion of the phenomenon of torture, admit being deeply troubled by how a democracy deals with the question of torture generally, let alone in the extreme example of the so-called "ticking time bomb" situation.

Until recently the question was hypothetical. It no longer is.

There are variations on the ticking time bomb situation, but the essence is in this plausible scenario: A known terrorist in FBI custody, whose information is credible, won't disclose where in Washington, DC, he has secreted a "weapon of mass destruction"—a nuclear bomb—set to detonate in two hours. The Bureau is certain that the terrorist will never voluntarily reveal the bomb's location. *In two hours our nation's capital could be wiped from the face of the earth, our government decimated, surrounding areas irredeemably contaminated, and the United States laid defenseless to unimaginable predation by our enemies.*

What to do?

The literature on torture is voluminous, most commentators concluding that torture is odious and unacceptable at all *times and under* all *circumstances, especially in a democracy. . . . But is it?*

Accepting these facts for the sake of argument, we have only two choices. Do nothing, and suffer the unimaginable consequences, or torture the information out of the terrorist.

There are those among us—[former U.S. president] Jimmy

Carter–like pacifists and [former U.S. attorney general] Ramsey Clark–type America haters come to mind—who would probably stand by idly and endure an atomic holocaust. But most people would doubtless opt for torture, albeit reluctantly.

These realists would be correct. They would be entitled to be free of even a scintilla of moral guilt, because torture—of whatever kind, and no matter how brutal—in defense of legitimate self-preservation is not only *not* immoral, *it is a moral imperative.*

The Jean Leon Case

Unknown to most Americans, one case in two different courts in the United States—a state appellate court in Florida, and a federal Court of Appeals—[has], albeit implicitly, endorsed such a use of physical force, and thus of torture, if necessary to save lives.

Jean Leon kidnapped one Louis Gachelin, who was held at gunpoint by Leon's accomplice. A ransom was arranged, a trap was sprung, and Leon was arrested.

> *Torture . . . in defense of legitimate self-preservation is not only* not *immoral,* it is a moral imperative.

Fearing that the accomplice would kill Gachelin if Leon didn't return promptly with the ransom money, the police demanded to know where the victim was being held. Leon wouldn't talk.

According to the Third District Court of Appeal of the State of Florida, when Leon "refused, he was set upon by several of the officers. They threatened and physically abused him by twisting his arm behind his back and choking him [and, allegedly, threatened to kill him] until he revealed where . . . [Gachelin] was being held. The officers went to the designated apartment, rescued . . . [Gachelin] and arrested . . . [the accomplice]."

Leon on Trial

While this was happening, Leon was taken "downtown," questioned by a different team of detectives, and informed of his

Miranda rights. He signed a waiver and confessed to the kidnapping. But before Leon's trial, he sought to exclude his police station confession, arguing that it was the tainted product of the cops' literal arm twisting, choking, and threats. (No self-incrimination issue arose from Leon having revealed the victim's location because that information was not sought to be used against him at his trial.)

The trial judge denied Leon's motion to suppress his confession on the ground that the force and threats used on him at the time of arrest *were not the reason for his confession.* In other words, the conceded coercion at the time of Leon's arrest had *dissipated* by the time of his confession, which the trial judge ruled had been given voluntarily.

Leon appealed. The Florida appeals court affirmed, reaching the same conclusion as the trial judge: Whatever had happened at Leon's arrest, the coercion had dissipated by the time he'd confessed. Thus, it was proper to use Leon's confession against him at trial.

That ruling should have been the end of Leon's first appeal because the only question in the case was the admissibility of Leon's confession. Yet the appeal court's opinion went further than the facts of the case required. In language lawyers call *dicta*—judicial reflections in no way necessary for a decision— the appellate judge added, gratuitously, that *"the force and threats asserted upon Leon in the parking lot were understandably motivated by the immediate necessity to find the victim and save his life."*

> *Unknown to most Americans, one case in two different courts in the United States . . . [has], albeit implicitly, endorsed [the] use of physical force, and thus of torture, if necessary to save lives.*

Consider the implications. Even though the motive for using force, and the police's use of it, were irrelevant to the decision, the appellate court's 2-1 majority saw fit to give its *express* approval of physical and psychological coercion in this situation, so long as the product of that coercion (the confession) was not used against defendant Leon at his trial.

Lest anyone think that the *dicta* in this decision was an

aberration, we need look only at the *unanimous* three-judge decision in Leon's further appeal to the United States Court of Appeals for the Eleventh Circuit.

> **❝** *Once the principle is accepted that torture legitimately can be employed to save lives—all that remains is the* application *of that principle to concrete cases.* **❞**

The facts were not in dispute. Once again, the only issue on appeal was whether the physical and psychological coercion at the time of arrest tainted the confession, or whether the coercion had, by then, sufficiently dissipated to make Leon's confession voluntary.

The Federal Court's Ruling

First, the federal appeals court dealt with self-incrimination. As to Leon's arrest statement concerning where his accomplice was holding Gachelin, there was no issue since the prosecution, properly, had never tried to introduce that statement at the trial. Next, whatever coercion had been used, it did not taint Leon's later confession because, according to the court, "the totality of the circumstances . . . clearly confirms . . . that the second statement was voluntary." Therefore, that statement was both voluntary and admissible.

The federal appeal court's ruling concerning the voluntariness of Leon's confession *completely disposed of the case*. But, as with the earlier appeal, this court took the unnecessary step of including *dicta* to the effect that the use of coercion at Leon's arrest was "motivated by the immediate necessity of finding the victim and saving his life," and that "this was a group of concerned officers acting in a reasonable manner to obtain information they needed in order to protect another individual from bodily harm or death."

All true. But, again, irrelevant to the sole question before the court as to whether the coercion used at the arrest had dissipated by the time of the confession.

Since the appellate courts, both state and federal, went out of their way to express their approval of coercion in a life-threatening situation, their *dicta* is noteworthy because it signals their acceptance of coercion *in principle*—a legitimization, as it were.

It is but a short step from arm twisting, choking, and death threats to the use of torture.

If, without objection from a state and a federal appeals court (indeed, with their apparent approval), the Florida police could employ a relatively benign form of coercion to save the life of a kidnap victim, it follows that the same rationale would support actual torture (physical and/or psychological) in a ticking time bomb situation.

Once *that* threshold is crossed—once the principle is accepted that torture legitimately can be employed to save lives—all that remains is the *application* of that principle to concrete cases. While that application could be difficult—requiring some form of probable cause, judicial oversight, and the like—the need to create such important procedural safeguards does not negate the argument that, in this country, where killers are routinely put to death for the commission of a single murder, it is neither immoral nor illegal *in principle* to employ non-lethal torture in the name of saving thousands of innocent American lives.

3

Torture Should Be Legalized and Regulated

Alan M. Dershowitz

Alan M. Dershowitz is professor of law at Harvard University. He is author of twenty-one books on a wide range of legal and social topics, including The Best Defense *(1982),* Letters to a Young Lawyer *(2001), and* Why Terrorism Works *(2002).*

In the wake of the September 11, 2001, terrorist attacks, many in the law enforcement community have been frustrated with their inability to collect information from suspected terrorists and material witnesses. The use of truth serum, moderate physical pressure, and torture are generally dismissed as unconstitutional, in spite of the fact that nothing in the Constitution explicitly forbids any of these techniques. It is a given that in any "ticking bomb" scenario where torture is the only way to prevent death, it will be used—either legally and transparently, or illegally and secretly. By giving judges the authority to issue special "torture warrants" in extreme cases, the U.S. government can include these inevitable scenarios within the context of U.S. law.

The FBI's frustration over its inability to get material witnesses to talk has raised a disturbing question rarely debated in this country: When, if ever, is it justified to resort to unconventional techniques such as truth serum, moderate physical pressure and outright torture?

The constitutional answer to this question may surprise people who are not familiar with the current U.S. Supreme Court interpretation of the 5th Amendment privilege against

Alan M. Dershowitz, "Commentary: Is There a Torturous Road to Justice?" *Los Angeles Times*, November 8, 2001. Copyright © 2001 by Alan M. Dershowitz. Reproduced by permission.

self-incrimination: Any interrogation technique, including the use of truth serum or even torture, is not prohibited. All that is prohibited is the introduction into evidence of the fruits of such techniques in a criminal trial against the person on whom the techniques were used. But the evidence could be used against that suspect in a non-criminal case—such as a deportation hearing—or against someone else.

If a suspect is given "use immunity"—a judicial decree announcing in advance that nothing the defendant says (or its fruits) can be used against him in a criminal case—he can be compelled to answer all proper questions. The issue then becomes what sorts of pressures can constitutionally be used to implement that compulsion.

We know that he can be imprisoned until he talks. But what if imprisonment is insufficient to compel him to do what he has a legal obligation to do? Can other techniques of compulsion be attempted?

Truth Serum and Constitutional Rights

Let's start with truth serum. What right would be violated if an immunized suspect who refused to comply with his legal obligation to answer questions truthfully were compelled to submit to an injection that made him do so?

Not his privilege against self-incrimination, since he has no such privilege now that he has been given immunity.

> *When, if ever, is it justified to resort to unconventional techniques such as truth serum, moderate physical pressure and outright torture?*

What about his right of bodily integrity? The involuntariness of the injection itself does not pose a constitutional barrier. No less a civil libertarian than Justice William J. Brennan rendered a decision that permitted an allegedly drunken driver to be involuntarily injected to remove blood for alcohol testing. Certainly there can be no constitutional distinction between an injection that removes a liquid and one that injects a liquid.

What about the nature of the substance injected? If it is relatively benign and creates no significant health risk, the only issue would be that it compels the recipient to do something he doesn't want to do. But he has a legal obligation to do precisely what the serum compels him to do: answer all questions truthfully.

> *// Torture in general certainly shocks the conscience of most civilized nations. But what if it were limited to . . . the situation in which a captured terrorist who knows of an imminent large-scale threat refuses to disclose it? //*

What if the truth serum doesn't work? Could the judge issue a "torture warrant," authorizing the FBI to employ specified forms of non-lethal physical pressure to compel the immunized suspect to talk?

Here we run into another provision of the Constitution—the due process clause, which may include a general "shock the conscience" test. And torture in general certainly shocks the conscience of most civilized nations.

But what if it were limited to the rare "ticking bomb" case—the situation in which a captured terrorist who knows of an imminent large-scale threat refuses to disclose it?

Would torturing one guilty terrorist to prevent the deaths of a thousand innocent civilians shock the conscience of all decent people?

To prove that it would not, consider a situation in which a kidnapped child had been buried in a box with two hours of oxygen. The kidnapper refuses to disclose its location. Should we not consider torture in that situation?

Regulating Torture

All of that said, the argument for allowing torture as an approved technique, even in a narrowly specified range of cases, is very troubling.

We know from experience that law enforcement personnel who are given limited authority to torture will expand its use. The cases that have generated the current debate over torture illustrate this problem. And, concerning the arrests made following the Sept. 11 attacks, there is no reason to believe that the detainees know about specific future terrorist targets. Yet there have been calls to torture these detainees.

I have no doubt that if an actual ticking bomb situation were to arise, our law enforcement authorities would torture. The real debate is whether such torture should take place outside of our legal system or within it. The answer to this seems clear: If we are to have torture, it should be authorized by the law.

Judges should have to issue a "torture warrant" in each case. Thus we would not be winking an eye of quiet approval at torture while publicly condemning it.

Democracy requires accountability and transparency, especially when extraordinary steps are taken. Most important, it requires compliance with the rule of law. And such compliance is impossible when an extraordinary technique, such as torture, operates outside of the law.

4

The U.S. Military Need Not Obey the Geneva Conventions When Dealing with Suspected Terrorists

John Yoo

John Yoo is professor of law at the University of California, Berkeley.

Following the Afghanistan War in late 2001 and early 2002, the United States detained hundreds of suspected Taliban and al Qaeda fighters in the U.S. military base hosted in Guantánamo Bay, Cuba. The administration of President George W. Bush held that these prisoners were enemy combatants rather than prisoners of war, and therefore did not fall under the statutes of the Geneva Conventions, a series of international laws regulating the treatment of war prisoners. This was the sensible thing to do, because the Taliban and al Qaeda fighters did not themselves adhere to the Geneva Conventions. The basis of the Geneva Conventions is mutual respect for the law—the United States obeys them primarily so that other countries that capture U.S. prisoners will also obey them. Furthermore, the statutes of the Geneva Conventions clearly state which combatants may qualify as prisoners of war: They must wear uniforms, have a clear command structure, and obey the laws of war. Neither al Qaeda nor the Taliban meet these requirements. It would be senseless to apply the Geneva Conventions in this context because their use is not mandated and would unduly restrict U.S. intelligence-gathering capabilities.

In light of the Abu Ghraib prison scandal [in which U.S. soldiers abused Iraqi prisoners], critics are arguing that abuses of Iraqi prisoners are being produced by a climate of disregard for the laws of war. Human-rights advocates, for example, claim that the mistreatment of Iraqi prisoners is of a piece with President [George W.] Bush's 2002 decision to deny al Qaeda and Taliban fighters the legal status of prisoners of war under the Geneva Conventions. Critics, no doubt, will soon demand that reforms include an extension of Geneva standards to interrogations at Guantanamo Bay [Cuba, where war-on-terror detainees are held].

> *The conflict with al Qaeda is not governed by the Geneva Conventions, which [apply] only to international conflicts between states that have signed them.*

The effort to blur the lines between Guantanamo and Abu Ghraib reflects a deep misunderstanding about the different legal regimes that apply to Iraq and the war against al Qaeda. It ignores the unique demands of the war on terrorism and the advantages that a facility such as Guantanamo can provide. It urges policy makers and the Supreme Court to make the mistake of curing what could prove to be an isolated problem by disarming the government of its principal weapon to stop future terrorist attacks. Punishing abuse in Iraq should not return the U.S. to Sept. 10, 2001, in the way it fights al Qaeda, while [terrorist leader] Osama bin Laden and his top lieutenants remain at large and continue to plan attacks.

A New Kind of War

It is important to recognize the differences between the war in Iraq and the war on terrorism. The treatment of those detained at Abu Ghraib is governed by the Geneva Conventions, which have been signed by both the U.S. and Iraq. President Bush and his commanders announced early in the conflict that the Conventions applied. Article 17 of the Third Geneva Convention, which applies to prisoners of war [POWs], clearly states: "No physical or mental torture, nor any other form of coercion, may be inflicted on prisoners of war to secure from them information of any kind whatever." This provision would prohibit some interrogation methods that could be used in American police stations.

One thing should remain clear. Physical abuse violates the Conventions. The armed forces have long operated a system designed to investigate violations of the laws of war, and ultimately to try and punish the offenders. And it is important to let the military justice system run its course. Article 5 of the Fourth Geneva Convention, which governs the treatment of civilians in occupied territories, states that if a civilian "is definitely suspected of or engaged in activities hostile to the security of the States, such individual person shall not be entitled to claim such rights and privileges under the present Convention as would, if exercised in favor of such individual person, be prejudicial to the security of such State." To be sure, Article 31 of the Fourth Convention prohibits any "physical or moral coercion" of civilians "to obtain information from them," and there is a clear prohibition of torture, physical abuse, and denial of medical care, food, and shelter. Nonetheless, Article 5 makes clear that if an Iraqi civilian who is not a member of the armed forces, has engaged in attacks on Coalition forces, the Geneva Convention permits the use of more coercive interrogation approaches to prevent future attacks.

> *The primary enforcer of the laws of war has been reciprocal treatment: We obey the Geneva Conventions because our opponent does the same with American POWs.*

A response to criminal action by individual soldiers should begin with the military justice system, rather than efforts to impose a one-size-fits-all policy to cover both Iraqi saboteurs and al Qaeda operatives. That is because the conflict with al Qaeda is not governed by the Geneva Conventions, which [apply] only to international conflicts between states that have signed them. Al Qaeda is not a nation-state, and its members—as they demonstrated so horrifically on Sept. 11, 2001—violate the very core principle of the laws of war by targeting innocent civilians for destruction. While Taliban [anti-U.S. Afghan] fighters had an initial claim to protection under the Conventions (since Afghanistan signed the treaties), they lost POW status by failing to obey the standards of conduct for legal combatants: wearing uniforms, a responsible command structure, and obeying the laws of war.

> *Applying different standards to al Qaeda does not abandon Geneva, but only recognizes that the U.S. faces a stateless enemy never contemplated by the Conventions.*

As a result, interrogations of detainees captured in the war on terrorism are not regulated under Geneva. This is not to condone torture, which is still prohibited by the Torture Convention and federal criminal law. Nonetheless, Congress's definition of torture in those laws—the infliction of severe mental or physical pain—leaves room for interrogation methods that go beyond polite conversation. Under the Geneva Convention, for example, a POW is required only to provide name, rank, and serial number and cannot receive any benefits for cooperating.

Fairness and Reciprocity

The reasons to deny Geneva status to terrorists extend beyond pure legal obligation. The primary enforcer of the laws of war has been reciprocal treatment: We obey the Geneva Conventions because our opponent does the same with American POWs. That is impossible with al Qaeda. It has never demonstrated any desire to provide humane treatment to captured Americans. If anything, the murders of [U.S. civilians] Nicholas Berg and Daniel Pearl declare al Qaeda's intentions to kill even innocent civilian prisoners. Without territory, it does not even have the resources to provide detention facilities for prisoners, even if it were interested in holding captured POWs.

It is also worth asking whether the strict limitations of Geneva make sense in a war against terrorists. Al Qaeda operates by launching surprise attacks on civilian targets with the goal of massive casualties. Our only means for preventing future attacks, which could use WMDs [weapons of mass destruction], is by acquiring information that allows for pre-emptive action. Once the attacks *occur*, as we learned on Sept. 11, it is too late. It makes little sense to deprive ourselves of an important, and legal, means to detect and prevent terrorist attacks while we are still in the middle of a fight to the death with al Qaeda. Applying different standards to al Qaeda does not abandon Geneva, but only recognizes that the U.S. faces a stateless enemy never contemplated by the Conventions.

This means that the U.S. can pursue different interrogation policies in each location. In fact, Abu Ghraib highlights the benefits of Guantanamo. We can guess that the unacceptable conduct of the soldiers at Abu Ghraib resulted in part from the dangerous state of affairs on the ground in a theater of war. American soldiers had to guard prisoners on the inside while receiving mortar and weapons fire from the outside. By contrast, Guantanamo is distant from any battlefield, making it far more secure. The naval station's location means the military can base more personnel there and devote more resources to training and supervision.

5

The U.S. Military Should Always Obey the Geneva Conventions

Lincoln Caplan

Lincoln Caplan is president and editor of Legal Affairs *magazine. He is also author of three books on legal topics, including* The Tenth Justice: The Solicitor General and the Rule of Law *(1987).*

The administration of President George W. Bush, acting in response to the terrorist attacks of September 11, 2001, has worked to classify terrorists as exempt from the Geneva Conventions, a set of international agreements that prohibit the torture and physical coercion of war prisoners. The logic the administration used was carried over in Iraq and reflected in the abuses at Abu Ghraib prison in Baghdad, where U.S. soldiers humiliated and physically coerced inmates. This demonstrates the dangers of making exceptions to the Geneva Conventions. Once it becomes acceptable to mistreat one group of prisoners, it will become easier to make it acceptable to mistreat other prisoners. The only way to ensure that the Geneva Conventions will be observed when they need to be is to observe them at all times.

The war in Iraq was sold to us as a moral undertaking. Even when the Bush Administration offered other rationales for the conflict, it positioned the United States as the liberator of an oppressed people from an immoral dictator. The photographs of systematic "inhumane and degrading treatment," as the In-

Lincoln Caplan, "War's Conventions," *Legal Affairs*, July/August 2004. Copyright © 2004 by *Legal Affairs*. Reproduced by permission.

ternational Red Cross called the cruelty at [U.S.-administered] Abu Ghraib [military prison in Baghdad, Iraq], shook this foundation. The brutal misuse of power by American guards over prisoners in their charge, some of it by deliberate physical abuse—torture—to help get information, was antithetical to our liberal democracy's special regard for individual rights. The images of Americans tormenting Iraqis in chambers once favored by [Iraqi dictator] Sadddam Hussein knocked our country off the moral pedestal it had built for itself.

The Geneva Conventions and the War on Terror

The Geneva Conventions were drafted in the wake of World War II to address deficiencies in the law of war, such as the inadequate protection of individuals under an enemy's sway and the lack of clarity about when that law's safeguards should apply. There are four conventions, or treaties, and the U.S. ratified them in 1955 and made them the law of the land. With its best-known prohibitions against "cruel treatment and torture" and "outrages upon personal dignity, in particular, humiliating and degrading treatment," the third convention spells out rules for the treatment of war prisoners.

> *The conventions may be the most solemn example of a set of rules so widely recognized that it would be unthinkable not to obey them as international law.*

Since [the terrorist attacks of] September 11 [2001] the administration has skirted the conventions where it could, most brazenly at the detention center in [the U.S. military prison of] Guantanamo Bay, Cuba. White House counsel Alberto Gonzalez claimed in a memo to President George W. Bush that the new war rendered the conventions' limits on interrogating prisoners "obsolete." In the blockbuster cases of the recent Supreme Court term, the court considered the due process owed to individuals captured in the war on terrorism. It further dealt with the administration's contention that these individuals are enemy combatants, not prisoners of war, and that they warrant scant protection under the Geneva rules as well as the Constitution.

Because the Bush Administration has treated the wars on terrorism and on Iraq as the same, it's remarkable that everyone in the chain of command who commented on the Abu Ghraib abuses, from Secretary of Defense Donald Rumsfeld and General Richard Myers, Chairman of the Joint Chiefs of Staff, on down, said that the Geneva Conventions apply. There were competing accounts about whether the soldiers were made aware of the rules: A U.S. military police reservist, Spec. Sabrina Harman, facing court martial for prisoner abuse said she never saw a copy of the conventions while serving as a guard. On the other hand, the head of Army intelligence, Lt. Gen. Keith Alexander, declared, "We train all our interrogators in the law and the Geneva Conventions, and they're held to that standard." However they were invoked, the conventions were treated as a given in a volatile state of affairs.

The Dangers of Flouting International Law

The conventions may be the most solemn example of a set of rules so widely recognized that it would be unthinkable not to obey them as international law. Including the United States, 191 countries have adopted them. Having tried to flout the conventions in its prosecution of the war on terrorism, the Bush Administration responded to the Iraq scandal by insisting on its deep commitment to the conventions and, more fundamentally, on its fidelity to international law as proof of its uprightness.

> **"** *Despite the Bush Administration's rhetoric about the Iraq war, its claims to moral purpose have often taken a back seat to bald assertions of American power.* **"**

The administration's record on major choices about international law belies that claim. President Bush set the tone early in his tenure by refusing to ratify the Kyoto Protocol for the reduction of greenhouse gas emissions, which the U.S. had already signed along with 83 other countries. He then withdrew President Bill Clinton's signature from the International Criminal Court treaty supported by 94 other countries. And, of course, he waged war on Iraq, which was arguably illegal because the United Nations resolutions that Bush relied on didn't authorize the use of force. This pattern has underscored the president's well-established habit of acting as if there's one standard for other nations and a different standard for the U.S., which we are free to choose instead because of our unrivaled power.

Despite the Bush Administration's rhetoric about the Iraq war, its claims to moral purpose have often taken a back seat to bald assertions of American power. The administration's approach to international law has exemplified this unilateralism and expediency. International law has moral force—whether or not it serves Bush's interests. But even by its own calculus of expediency, the administration should have proclaimed its obedience to the Geneva Conventions earlier and more often, so that when the time came to apportion responsibility for what happened at Abu Ghraib, the question wouldn't be what orders were given—but why they were disregarded.

6

"Stress and Duress" Techniques Are Forms of Torture

Tom Malinowski

Tom Malinowski is Washington, D.C., advocacy director for Human Rights Watch, an international organization that promotes human rights.

The administration of President George W. Bush has used physical coercion to physically and mentally weaken suspected terrorists without technically torturing them. These techniques include stripping prisoners, forcing them to maintain uncomfortable physical positions for long periods of time, exposing them to heat and cold, depriving them of food and sleep, and using other means to break their will. The fact that these forms of physical coercion are severe enough to actually result in new information clearly indicates that they inflict enough suffering to qualify as torture. If they did not, prisoners would have no reason to submit to their interrogators' demands.

"I stand for 8–10 hours a day. Why is [forced] standing [for prisoners] limited to four hours?"

So reads a note scrawled by Defense Secretary Donald Rumsfeld on a memo released by the Pentagon [in June 2004], in which he approved for [U.S.] Guantanamo [Bay, Cuba, where war-on-terror detainees are held] interrogation techniques such as forcing them to stand, stripping detainees nude and threatening them with dogs.

Gentle Torture

With his characteristic cut-through-the-bull bluntness, Rumsfeld raised a valid question. If interrogators can use methods designed to inflict pain on prisoners, why should they be made to stop before the pain becomes difficult to bear? After all, forcing a prisoner to stand, so long as it's only for a short time, is a bit like allowing the use of hot irons, so long as they're only slightly above room temperature. The contradiction Rumsfeld noticed may help us understand how decisions made by senior officials and military commanders led to the abuse of prisoners in Abu Ghraib [military prison in U.S.-occupied Iraq].

The policymakers apparently tried to have it both ways, approving highly coercive interrogation techniques, but with limits designed to assuage their consciences and satisfy their lawyers. They authorized or proposed painful "stress positions," but said that no one position could be used for more than 45 minutes. They allowed forced standing, but only for four hours; sleep deprivation, but only for 72 hours; exposure to heat and cold, but with medical monitoring; hooding, but not in a way that limits breathing; and nudity, but not the stacking of nude bodies.

Once these methods were applied in the field on prisoners considered to be hardened terrorists, however, interrogators did not respect the lawyers' boundaries. Indeed, they could not have respected them while still achieving their aim of forcing information from detainees. For by definition, these methods, euphemistically known as "stress and duress," can work only when applied beyond the limits of a prisoner's tolerance.

> *Torture works only (if ever) when it truly feels like torture.*

Perhaps one reason these stress and duress techniques were approved at all is that they sound innocuous. But as anyone who has worked with torture victims knows, they are the stock in trade of brutal regimes around the world. For example, the

Washington Times recently reported that "some of the most feared forms of torture cited" by survivors of the North Korean gulag [prison camp] "were surprisingly mundane: Guards would force inmates to stand perfectly still for hours at a time, or make them perform exhausting repetitive exercises such as standing up and sitting down until they collapsed from fatigue."

> *It's not likely anyone was holding a stopwatch during this treatment or making sure that only 'mild' pain and suffering resulted. Why would they have?*

Binding prisoners in painful positions is a torture technique widely used in countries such as China and Burma, and repeatedly condemned by the United States. Stripping Muslim prisoners nude to humiliate them was a common practice of the Soviet military when it occupied Afghanistan [during the 1980s]. As for sleep deprivation, consider former Israeli Prime Minister Menachem Begin's account of experiencing it in a Soviet prison in the 1940s:

> In the head of the interrogated prisoner a haze begins to form. His spirit is wearied to death, his legs are unsteady, and he has one sole desire: to sleep, to sleep just a little, not to get up, to lie, to rest, to forget. . . . Anyone who has experienced this desire knows that not even hunger or thirst are comparable with it. . . . I came across prisoners who signed what they were ordered to sign, only to get what the interrogator promised them. He did not promise them their liberty. He promised them—if they signed—uninterrupted sleep!

The Purpose of Pain

Rumsfeld eventually rescinded his approval of these cruel methods for Guantanamo. But they still ended up being authorized by commanders and used on prisoners throughout Afghanistan and Iraq. Former detainees report being forced to stand, sit or crouch for many hours, often in contorted positions, deprived of sleep for nights on end, held nude, doused with cold water and exposed to extreme heat.

It's not likely anyone was holding a stopwatch during this treatment or making sure that only "mild" pain and suffering resulted. Why would they have? For the limits that might have made the treatment more humane would also have rendered it ineffective in the eyes of interrogators.

Stress and duress interrogation techniques were invented in the dungeons of the world's most brutal regimes for only one purpose—to cause pain, distress and humiliation, without physical scars. When Bush administration officials and military commanders told soldiers to use methods designed for that purpose, while still treating detainees "humanely," they were being naive at best and dishonest at worst. They should have known that once the purpose of inflicting pain is legitimized, those charged with the care and interrogation of prisoners will take it to its logical conclusion.

7

"Stress and Duress" Techniques Are Legitimate Forms of Interrogation

Mark Bowden

Mark Bowden is a staff writer for the Philadelphia Inquirer. *He is author of seven books, including the best-selling* Black Hawk Down: A Story of Modern War *(1999).*

The use of physical coercion and discomfort in interrogating high-level terrorists is justified, provided that it does not rise to the level of torture. The capture of al Qaeda terrorist leader Khalid Sheikh Mohammed, who helped plan the terrorist attacks of September 11, 2001, is an excellent example of a case where these interrogation techniques would be justified. Although those subjected to physical coercion and discomfort are unlikely to react immediately, the long-term psychological effects render suspected terrorist leaders more vulnerable to traditional interrogation techniques.

On what may or may not have been a Saturday, on what may have been March 1 [2003], in a house in this city that may have been this squat two-story white one belonging to [Pakistani citizen] Ahmad Abdul Qadoos, with big gray-headed crows barking in the front yard, the notorious terrorist Khalid Sheikh Mohammed was roughly awakened by a raiding party of Pakistani and American commandos. Anticipating a gunfight, they entered loud and fast. Instead they found him asleep. He was pulled from [his] bed, hooded, bound, hustled from the house, placed in a vehicle, and driven quickly away.

> **❝** *[Sheikh Mohammed] would most likely have been locked naked in a cell with no traces of daylight. The space would be filled night and day with harsh light and noise, and would be so small that he would be unable to stand upright.* **❞**

Here was the biggest catch yet in the war on terror. Sheikh Mohammed is considered the architect of two attempts on the World Trade Center: the one that failed, in 1993, and the one that succeeded so catastrophically, eight years later [in the attacks of September 11, 2001]. He is also believed to have been behind the attacks on the U.S. embassies in Kenya and Tanzania in 1998, and on the USS *Cole* two years later, and behind the slaughter [in 2002] of the *Wall Street Journal* reporter Daniel Pearl, among other things. An intimate of [terrorist leader] Osama bin Laden's, Sheikh Mohammed has been called the operations chief of al-Qaeda, if such a formal role can be said to exist in such an informal organization. Others have suggested that an apter designation might be al-Qaeda's "chief franchisee." Whatever the analogy, he is one of the terror organization's most important figures, a burly, distinctly modern, cosmopolitan thirty-seven-year-old man fanatically devoted to a medieval form of Islam. He was born to Pakistani parents, raised in Kuwait, and educated in North Carolina to be an engineer before he returned to the Middle East to build a career of bloody mayhem.

The Mastermind

Some say that Sheikh Mohammed was captured months before the March 1 date announced by Pakistan's Inter-Services Intelligence (ISI). Abdul Qadoos, a pale, white-bearded alderman in this well-heeled neighborhood, told me that Sheikh Mohammed was not there "then or ever." The official video of the takedown appears to have been faked. But the details are of minor importance. Whenever, wherever, and however it happened, nearly everyone now agrees that Sheikh Mohammed is in U.S. custody, and has been for some time. In the first hours of his captivity the hood came off and a picture was taken. It shows a bleary-eyed, heavy, hairy, swarthy man with a full black moustache, thick eyebrows, a dark outline of beard on a rounded, shaved face, three chins, long sideburns, and a full head of dense, long, wildly mussed black hair. He stands before a pale tan wall whose paint is chipped, leaning slightly forward, like a man with his hands bound behind him, the low cut of his loose-fitting white T-shirt exposing matted curls of hair on his chest, shoulders, and back. He is looking down and to the right of the camera. He appears dazed and glum.

Sheikh Mohammed is a smart man. There is an anxious, searching quality to his expression in that first past-arrest photo. It is the look of a man awakened into nightmare. Everything that has given [his] life meaning, his role as husband and father, his leadership, his stature, plans, and ambitions, is finished. His future is months, maybe years, of imprisonment and interrogation; a military tribunal; and almost certain execution. You can practically see the wheels turning in his head, processing his terminal predicament. How will he spend his last months and years? Will he maintain a dignified, defiant silence? Or will he succumb to his enemy and betray his friends, his cause, and his faith?

> *Isolated, confused, weary, hungry, frightened, and tormented, Sheikh Mohammed would gradually be reduced to a seething collection of simple needs. . . . The key to filling all those needs would be the same: to talk.*

If Sheikh Mohammed felt despair in those first hours, it didn't show. According to a Pakistani officer who sat in on an initial ISI questioning, the al-Qaeda sub-boss seemed calm and stoic. For his first two days in custody he said nothing beyond confirming his name. A CIA [Central Intelligence Agency] official says that Sheikh Mohammed spent those days "sitting in a trancelike state and reciting verses from the Koran [the holy book of Islam]." On the third day he is said to have loosened up. Fluent in the local languages of Urdu, Pashto, and Baluchi, he tried to shame his Pakistani interrogators, lecturing them on their responsibilities as Muslims and upbraiding them for co-operating with infidels.

"Playing an American surrogate won't help you or your country," he said. "There are dozens of people like me who will give their lives but won't let the Americans live in peace anywhere in the world." Asked if Osama bin Laden was alive, he said, "Of course he is alive." He spoke of meeting with bin Laden in "a mountainous border region" in December [2002]. He seemed smug about U.S. and British preparations for war against [Iraqi dictator] Saddam Hussein. "Let the Iraq War begin," he said. "The U.S. forces will be targeted inside their bases in the [Persian Gulf]. I don't have any specific information, but my sixth sense is telling me that you will get the news from Saudi Arabia, Qatar, and Kuwait." Indeed, in the following months al-Qaeda carried out a murderous attack in Saudi Arabia.

On that third day, once more hooded, Sheikh Mohammed was driven to Chaklala Air Force base, in Rawalpindi, and turned over to U.S. forces. From there he was flown to the CIA interrogation center in Bagram, Afghanistan, and from there, some days later, to an "undisclosed location" (a place the CIA calls "Hotel California")—presumably a facility in another co-operative nation, or perhaps a specially designed prison aboard an aircraft carrier. It doesn't much matter where, because the place would not have been familiar or identifiable to him. Place and time, the anchors of sanity, were about to come unmoored. He might as well have been entering a new dimension, a strange new world where his every word, move, and sensation would be monitored and measured; where things might be as they seemed but might not; where there would be no such thing as day or night, or normal patterns of eating and drinking, wakefulness and sleep; where hot and cold, wet and dry, clean and dirty, truth and lies, would all be tangled and distorted.

Sheikh Mohammed in Prison

Intelligence and military officials would talk about Sheikh Mohammed's state only indirectly, and conditionally. But by the time he arrived at a more permanent facility, he would already have been bone-tired, hungry, sore, uncomfortable, and afraid—if not for himself, then for his wife and children, who had been arrested either with him or some months before, depending on which story you believe. He would have been warned that lack of cooperation might mean being turned over to the more direct and brutal interrogators of some third nation. He would most likely have been locked naked in a cell with no trace of daylight. The space would be filled night and day with harsh light and noise, and would be so small that he would be unable to stand upright, to sit comfortably, or to recline fully. He would be kept awake, cold, and probably wet. If he managed to doze, he would be roughly awakened. He would be fed infrequently and irregularly, and then only with thin, tasteless meals. Sometimes days would go by between periods of questioning, sometimes only hours or minutes. The human mind craves routine, and can adjust to almost anything in the presence of it, so his jailers would take care that no semblance of routine developed.

> *There are those who would applaud [Sheikh Mohammed's] principled defiance in captivity. But we pay for his silence in blood.*

Questioning would be intense—sometimes loud and rough, sometimes quiet and friendly, with no apparent reason for either. He would be questioned sometimes by one person, sometimes by two or three. The session might last for days, with interrogators taking turns, or it might last only a few minutes. He would be asked the same questions again and again, and then suddenly be presented with something completely unexpected—a detail or a secret that he would be shocked to find they knew. He would be offered the opportunity to earn freedom or better treatment for his wife and children. Whenever he was helpful and the information he gave proved true, his harsh conditions would ease. If the information proved false, his treatment would worsen. On occasion he might be given a drug to elevate his mood prior to interrogation; marijuana, heroin, and sodium pentothal have been shown to overcome a reluctance to speak, and methamphetamine can unleash a torrent of talk in the stubbornest subjects, the very urgency of the chatter making a complex lie impossible to sustain. These drugs could be administered surreptitiously with food or drink, and given the bleakness of his existence, they might even offer a brief period of relief and pleasure, thereby creating a whole new category of longing—and new leverage for his interrogators.

Deprived of any outside information, Sheikh Mohammed would grow more and more vulnerable to manipulation. For instance, intelligence gleaned after successful al-Qaeda attacks in Kuwait and Saudi Arabia might be fed to him, in bits and pieces, so as to suggest foiled operations. During questioning he would be startled regularly by details about his secret organization—details drawn from ongoing intelligence operations, new arrests, or the interrogation of other captive al-Qaeda members. Some of the information fed to him would be true, some of it false. Key associates might be said to be cooperating, or to have completely recanted their allegiance to jihad [holy struggle; in this case a reference to war]. As time went by, his knowledge would decay while that of his questioners improved. He might come to see once-vital plans as insignificant, or already known. The importance of certain secrets would gradually erode.

> *As these interrogators see it, the well-being of the captive must be weighed against the lives that might be saved by forcing him to talk.*

Isolated, confused, weary, hungry, frightened, and tormented, Sheikh Mohammed would gradually be reduced to a seething collection of simple needs, all of them controlled by his interrogators.

The key to filling all those needs would be the same: to talk.

Looking at Torture

We hear a lot these days about America's over-powering military technology; about the professionalism of its warriors; about the sophistication of its weaponry, eavesdropping, and telemetry; but right now the most vital weapon in its arsenal may well be the art of interrogation. To counter an enemy who relies on stealth and surprise, the most valuable tool is information, and often the only source of that information is the enemy himself. Men like Sheikh Mohammed who have been taken alive in this war are classic candidates for the most cunning practices of this dark art. Intellectual, sophisticated, deeply religious, and well trained, they present a perfect challenge for the interrogator. Getting at the information they possess could allow us to thwart major attacks, unravel their organization, and save thousands of lives. They and their situation pose one of the strongest arguments in modern times for the use of torture.

> *All [terrorism] suspects are questioned rigorously, but those in the top ranks get the full coercive treatment. And if official and unofficial government reports are to be believed, the methods work.*

Torture is repulsive. It is deliberate cruelty, a crude and ancient tool of political oppression. It is commonly used to terrorize people, or to wring confessions out of suspected criminals who may or may not be guilty. It is the classic shortcut for a lazy or incompetent investigator. Horrifying examples of torturers' handiwork are catalogued and publicized annually by [human rights groups such as] Amnesty International, Human Rights Watch, and other organizations that battle such abuses worldwide. One cannot help sympathizing with the innocent, powerless victims showcased in their literature. But professional terrorists pose a harder question. They are lockboxes containing potentially life-saving information. Sheikh Mohammed has his own political and religious reasons for plotting mass murder, and there are those who would applaud his principled defiance in captivity. But we pay for his silence in blood.

The word "torture" comes from the Latin verb torquere, "to twist." Webster's New World Dictionary offers the following primary definition: "The inflicting of severe pain to force information and confession, get revenge, etc." Note the adjective "severe," which summons up images of the rack, thumbscrews, gouges, branding irons, burning pits, impaling devices, electric shock, and all the other devilish tools devised by human beings to mutilate and inflict pain on others. All manner of innovative cruelty is still common-place, particularly in Central and South America, Africa, and the Middle East. [Iraqi dictator] Saddam Hussein's police force burned various marks into the foreheads of thieves and deserters, and routinely sliced tongues out of those whose words offended the state. In Sri Lanka prisoners are hung upside down and burned with hot irons. In China they are beaten with clubs and shocked with cattle prods. In India the police stick pins through the fingernails and fingers of prisoners. Maiming and physical abuse are legal in Somalia, Iran, Saudi Arabia, Nigeria, Sudan, and other countries that practice sharia [a strict interpretation of Islamic law]: the hands of thieves are lopped off, and women convicted of adultery may be stoned to death. Governments around the world continue to employ rape and mutilation, and to harm family members, including children, in order to extort confessions or information from those in captivity. Civilized people everywhere readily condemn these things.

"Torture Lite"

Then there are methods that, some people argue, fall short of torture. Called "torture lite," these include sleep deprivation, exposure to heat or cold, the use of drugs to cause confusion, rough treatment (slapping, shoving, or shaking), forcing a prisoner to stand for days at a time or to sit in uncomfortable positions, and playing on his fears for himself and his family. Although excruciating for the victim, these tactics generally leave no permanent marks and do no lasting physical harm.

> *It may be clear that coercion is sometimes the right choice, but how does one allow it yet still control it?*

The [international] Geneva Convention [regulating the treatment of war prisoners] makes no distinction: it bans any mistreatment of prisoners. But some nations that are otherwise committed to ending brutality have employed torture lite under what they feel are justifiable circumstances. In 1987 Israel attempted to codify a distinction between torture, which was banned, and "moderate physical pressure," which was permitted in special cases. Indeed, some police officers, soldiers, and intelligence agents who abhor "severe" methods believe that banning all forms of physical pressure would be dangerously naive. Few support the use of physical pressure to extract confessions, especially because victims will often say anything (to the point of falsely incriminating themselves) to put an end to pain. But many veteran interrogators believe that the use of such methods to extract information is justified if it could save lives—whether by forcing an enemy soldier to reveal his army's battlefield positions or forcing terrorists to betray the details of ongoing plots. As these interrogators see it, the well-being of the captive must be weighed against the lives that might be saved by forcing him to talk. A method that produces life-saving information without doing lasting harm to anyone is not just preferable; it appears to be morally sound. Hereafter I will use "torture" to mean the more severe traditional outrages, and "coercion" to refer to torture lite, or moderate physical pressure. . . .

> **"** *If making a man sit in a tiny chair that forces him to hang painfully by his bound hands when he slides forward is okay, then what about applying a little pressure to the base of his neck to aggravate that pain?* **"**

All [terrorism] suspects are questioned rigorously, but those in the top ranks get the full coercive treatment. And if official and unofficial government reports are to be believed, the methods work. In report after report hard-core terrorist leaders are said to be either cooperating or, at the very least, providing some information—not just vague statements but detailed, verifiable, useful intelligence. In late March [2003], *Time* reported that Sheikh Mohammed had "given U.S. interrogators the names and descriptions of about a dozen key al-Qaeda operatives believed to be plotting terrorist attacks on America and other western countries" and had "added crucial details to the descriptions of other suspects and filled in important gaps in what U.S. intelligence knows about al-Qaeda's practices." In June [2003], news reports suggested that Sheikh Mohammed was discussing operational planning with his captors and had told interrogators that al-Qaeda did not work with Saddam Hussein. And according to a report in June of [2002] [terrorist leader] Abu Zubaydah, who is said to be held in solitary confinement somewhere in Pakistan, provided information that helped foil a plot to detonate a radioactive bomb in the United States.

Secretary of Defense Donald Rumsfeld said in September [2002] that interrogation of captured terrorist leaders had yielded "an awful lot of information" and had "made life an awful lot more difficult for an awful lot of folks." Indeed, if press accounts can be believed, these captured Islamist fanatics are all but dismantling their own secret organization. According to published reports, Sheikh Mohammed was found in part because of information from [terrorist leader Ramzi] bin al-Shibh, whose arrest had been facilitated by information from Abu Zubaydah. Weeks after the sheikh's capture Bush Administration officials and intelligence experts told *The Washington Post* that the al-Qaeda deputy's "cooperation under interrogation" had given them hopes of arresting or killing the rest of the organization's top leadership.

A Skeptical Response

How much of this can be believed? Are such reports wishful thinking, or deliberate misinformation? There is no doubt that intelligence agencies have scored big victories over al-Qaeda in the past two years, but there is no way to corroborate these stories. President Bush himself warned, soon after 9/11, that in war mode his Administration would closely guard intelligence sources and methods. It would make sense to claim that top al-Qaeda leaders had caved under questioning even if they had not. Hard men like Abu Zubaydah, bin al-Shibh, and Sheikh Mohammed are widely admired in parts of the world. Word that they had been broken would demoralize their followers, and would encourage lower-ranking members of their organization to talk; if their leaders had given in, why should they hold out?

To some, all this jailhouse cooperation smells concocted. "I doubt we're getting very much out of them, despite what you read in the press," says a former CIA agent with experience in South America. "Everybody in the world knows that if you are arrested by the United States, nothing bad will happen to you."

Bill Cowan, a retired Marine lieutenant colonel who conducted interrogations in Vietnam, says, "I don't see the proof in the pudding. If you had a top leader like Mohammed talking, someone who could presumably lay out the whole organization for you, I think we'd be seeing sweeping arrests in several different countries at the same time. Instead what we see is an arrest here, then a few months later an arrest there."

These complaints are all from people who have no qualms about using torture to get information from men like Sheikh Mohammed. Their concern is that merely using coercion amounts to handling terrorists with kid gloves [that is, gently]. But the busts of al-Qaeda cells worldwide, and the continuing roundup of al-Qaeda leaders, suggest that some of those in custody are being made to talk. This worries people who campaign against all forms of torture. They believe that the rules are being ignored. Responding to rumors of mistreatment at [U.S. bases] Bagram [in Afghanistan] and Guantanamo [Bay, Cuba], Amnesty International and Human Rights Watch have written letters and met with Bush Administration officials. They haven't been able to learn much.

> **As long as it remains illegal to torture, the interrogator who employs coercion must accept the risk.**

Is the United States torturing prisoners? Three inmates have died in U.S. custody in Afghanistan, and reportedly eighteen prisoners at Guantanamo have attempted suicide; one prisoner there survived after hanging himself but remains unconscious and is not expected to revive. Shah Muhammad, a twenty-year-old Pakistani who was held at Camp X-Ray [the U.S. military base in Guantanamo Bay, Cuba] for eighteen months, told me that he repeatedly tried to kill himself in despair. "They were driving me crazy," he said. Public comments by Administration officials have fueled further suspicion. An unnamed intelligence official told *The Wall Street Journal*, "What's needed is a little bit of smacky-face. Some al-Qaeda just need some extra encouragement." Then there was the bravado of Cofer Black, the counterterrorism coordinator, in his congressional testimony last year. A pudgy, balding, round-faced man with glasses, who had served with the CIA before taking the State Department position, Black refused to testify behind a screen, as others had done. "The American people need to see my face," he said. "I want to look the American people in the eye." By way of presenting his credentials he said that in 1995 a group of "Osama bin Laden's thugs" were caught planning "to kill me.". . .

Serious interrogation is clearly being reserved for only the most dangerous men, like Sheikh Mohammed. So why not lift the fig leaf covering the use of coercion? Why not eschew hypocrisy, clearly define what is meant by the word "severe" and amend bans on torture to allow interrogators to coerce information from would-be terrorists?

This is the crux of the problem. It may be clear that coercion is sometimes the right choice, but how does one allow it yet still control it? Sadism is deeply rooted in the human psyche. Every army has its share of soldiers who delight in kicking and beating bound captives. Men in authority tend to abuse it—not all men, but many. As a mass, they should be assumed to lean toward abuse. How does a country best regulate behavior in its dark and distant corners, in prisons, on battlefields, and in interrogation rooms, particularly when its forces number in the millions and are spread all over the globe? In considering a change in national policy, one is obliged to anticipate the practical consequences. So if we formally lift the ban on torture, even if only partially and in rare, specific cases (the attorney and author Alan Dershowitz has proposed issuing "torture warrants"), the question will be, How can we ensure that the practice does not become commonplace—not just a tool for extracting vital, life-saving information in rare cases but a routine tool of oppression?

The Israeli Precedent

As it happens, a pertinent case study exists. Israel has been a target of terror attacks for many years, and has wrestled openly with the dilemmas they pose for a democracy. In 1987 a commission led by the retired Israeli Supreme Court justice Moshe Landau wrote a series of recommendations for Michael Koubi and his agents, allowing them to use "moderate physical pressure" and "nonviolent psychological pressure" in interrogating prisoners who had information that could prevent impending terror attacks. The commission sought to allow such coercion only in "ticking-bomb scenarios"—that is, in cases like the kidnapping of Jakob von Metzler, when the information withheld by the suspect could save lives.

Twelve years later the Israeli Supreme Court effectively revoked this permission, banning the use of any and all forms of torture. In the years following the Landau Commission recommendations, the use of coercive methods had become widespread in the Occupied Territories. It was estimated that more than two thirds of the Palestinians taken into custody were subjected to them. Koubi says that only in rare instances, and with court permission, did he slap, pinch, or shake a prisoner—but he happens to be an especially gifted interrogator. What about the hundreds of men who worked for him? Koubi could not be present for all those interrogations. Every effort to regulate coercion failed. In the abstract it was easy to imagine a ticking-bomb situation, and a suspect who clearly warranted rough treatment. But in real life where was the line to be drawn? Should coercive methods be applied only to someone who knows of an immediately pending attack? What about one who might know of attacks planned for months or years in the future?

> *It is wise of the President to reiterate U.S. support for international agreements banning torture, and it is wise for American interrogators to employ whatever coercive methods work.*

"Assuming you get useful information from torture, then why not always use torture?" asks Jessica Montell, the executive director of B'Tselem, a human-rights advocacy group in Jerusalem. "Why stop at the bomb that's already been planted and at people who know where the explosives are? Why not people who are building the explosives, or people who are donating money, or transferring the funds for the explosives? Why stop at the victim himself? Why not torture the victims' families, their relatives, their neighbors? If the end justifies the means, then where would you draw the line?"

And how does one define "coercion," as opposed to "torture"? If making a man sit in a tiny chair that forces him to hang painfully by his bound hands when he slides forward is okay, then what about applying a little pressure to the base of his neck to aggravate that pain? When does shaking or pushing a prisoner, which can become violent enough to kill or seriously injure a man, cross the line from coercion to torture?

Montell has thought about these questions a lot. She is thirty-five, a slender woman with scruffy short brown hair, who seems in perpetual motion, directing B'Tselem and tending baby twins and a four-year-old at home. Born in California, she emigrated to Israel partly out of feelings of solidarity with the Jewish state and partly because she found a job she liked in the human-rights field. Raised with a kind of idealized notion of Israel, she now seems committed to making the country live up to her ideals. But those ideals are hardheaded. Although Montell and her organization have steadfastly opposed the use of coercion (which she considers torture), she recognizes that the moral issue involved is not a simple one.

Torture and Coercion

She knows that the use of coercion in interrogation did not end completely when the Israeli Supreme Court banned it in 1999. The difference is that when interrogators use "aggressive methods" now, they know they are breaking the law and could potentially be held responsible for doing so. This acts as a deterrent, and tends to limit the use of coercion to only the most defensible situations.

"If I as an interrogator feel that the person in front of me has information that can prevent a catastrophe from happening," she says, "I imagine that I would do what I would have to do in order to prevent that catastrophe from happening. The state's obligation is then to put me on trial, for breaking the law. Then I come and say these are the facts that I had at my disposal. This is what I believed at the time. This is what I thought necessary to do. I can evoke the defense of necessity, and then the court decides whether or not it's reasonable that I broke the law in order to avert this catastrophe. But it has to be that I broke the law. It can't be that there's some prior license for me to abuse people."

In other words, when the ban is lifted, there is no restraining lazy, incompetent, or sadistic interrogators. As long as it remains illegal to torture, the interrogator who employs coercion must accept the risk. He must be prepared to stand up in court, if necessary, and defend his actions. Interrogators will still use coercion because in some cases they will deem it worth the consequences. This does not mean they will necessarily be punished. In any nation the decision to prosecute a crime is an executive one. A prosecutor, a grand jury, or a judge must decide to press charges, and the chances that an interrogator in a genuine ticking-bomb case would be prosecuted, much less convicted, is very small. . . .

The Bush Administration has adopted exactly the right posture on the matter. Candor and consistency are not always public virtues. Torture is a crime against humanity, but coercion is an issue that is rightly handled with a wink, or even a touch of hypocrisy; it should be banned but also quietly practiced. Those who protest coercive methods will exaggerate their horrors, which is good: it generates a useful climate of fear. It is wise of the President to reiterate U.S. support for international agreements banning torture, and it is wise for American interrogators to employ whatever coercive methods work. It is also smart not to discuss the matter with anyone.

If interrogators step over the line from coercion to outright torture, they should be held personally responsible. But no interrogator is ever going to be prosecuted for keeping Khalid Sheikh Mohammed awake, cold, alone, and uncomfortable. Nor should he be.

8

The Use of Torture Serves Current U.S. Foreign Policy Objectives

Glen T. Martin

Glen T. Martin is professor of philosophy and religious studies at Radford University, president of International Philosophers for Peace, president of the World Constitution and Parliament Association, and vice president of the Institute on World Problems.

The use of torture is an essential part of maintaining any empire, and the United States has been an empire since World War II. In the past it has promoted or sanctioned torture or other atrocities in many countries including Cambodia, Chile, El Salvador, Guatemala, Indonesia, Iran, Laos, Nicaragua, Panama, South Korea, and Vietnam. It has also produced numerous torturers and assassins at the controversial School of the Americas in Fort Benning, Georgia. The use of torture and other atrocities terrifies the populations of countries that serve U.S. interests, which allows the United States to consolidate wealth in its own native corporations, maintaining its power. The atrocities at Baghdad's Abu Ghraib prison, in which U.S. soldiers tortured Iraqi prisoners, is but the most recent example in a long pattern of U.S.-sanctioned torture and state-sponsored terrorism.

Glen T. Martin, "The Logic of Empire and Logic of Torture Essential to American Policy," *The Roanoke Times*, May 26, 2004. Copyright © 2004 by *The Roanoke Times*. Reproduced by permission of the author.

The furor about the U.S. use of torture arising from the revelations [detailing the abuse of Iraqi prisoners by U.S. soldiers] at Abu Ghraib prison has resulted in continuing revelations of similar forms of abuse in U.S. prisons, in Afghanistan, Guantanamo [Bay, Cuba, where detainees are being held] and elsewhere. It has also resulted in excellent articles about "Foolish dreams of American empire" like the editorial from *The Roanoke Times* on May 14 [2004].

This editoral pointed out that "empires require cruelty to subdue restive foreign populations." This is exactly to the point—the lust for empire and torture are inseparable. They go together.

> *The lust for empire and torture are inseparable. They go together.*

However, what has been slow in emerging from the furor about torture is recognition that the United States has been a global empire at least since World War II. The United States has acted to place itself at the center of a global empire directed toward controlling the wealth-producing process worldwide and guiding wealth and cheap raw materials into the hands of the world's dominant corporations.

The United States emerged from the war as the world's superpower, since all the contender industrial powers (Britain, France, Russia, Germany and Japan) had been devastated by the war. Postwar planners in their then-top-secret documents sketched out a postwar strategy that included U.S. control of a "grand area" (that included most of the world) that was to be a service area for U.S. investments, resources and cheap labor.

Documents such as *State Department Policy Planning Study No. 23* (1948) announced that in order to "maintain the disparity" in wealth in relation to the rest of the world, the U.S. government would have to "cease to talk about vague and . . . unreal objectives such as human rights, the raising of living standards, and democratization."

From now on it would have to "deal in straight power concepts." The planners understood that "straight power concepts" meant torture, military destruction of peoples who resisted, overthrow of democratic governments and police repression throughout the "grand area."

A History of Oppression

This is borne out in the factual record. Already, when the U.S. military entered Korea in 1945 before the Korean War, it forcibly removed the local government and instituted a puppet dictatorship in South Korea at the cost of murdering about 100,000 people.

Soon the CIA and U.S. military were engaged in brutally securing the "grand area" of the empire. We overthrew the democratic government of Iran in 1953 and placed in power the shah [king] of Iran, who was infamous for his use of torture. We overthrew the democratic government of Guatemala in 1954 and installed a military junta [dictatorship] that tortured and murdered about 200,000 Guatemalans during the next 40 years.

[During the Vietnam War] we installed a merciless dictatorship in South Vietnam and bombed Cambodia and Laos to ribbons during the 1960s, the U.S. military using torture, massacre and extermination bombings of defenseless villages routinely in Southeast Asia through its withdrawal in 1975.

> **//** It is important to realize that use of torture is not just for information. Its use is integral to the primary necessity of empire—to create terror in subject populations. **//**

Then–Secretary of Defense Robert McNamara stated in a famous speech on U.S. television that "Asian people don't respect human life the way we do." This sounds very much like [U.S. Defense Secretary] Donald Rumsfeld and [President] George [W.] Bush, who recently stated that a few bad soldiers do not reflect "the goodness of the American people."

The United States engineered a coup in Indonesia in 1965 that brought the brutal dictator [Mohamed] Suharto to power at the cost of half a million lives and routine torture of dissidents. In the U.S.-backed coup in Chile in 1973 (that destroyed Chilean democracy), the sports stadium in Santiago de Chile was immediately turned into a torture center with horrible sexual and gruesome forms of torture routinely applied to all prisoners. Very similar to Abu Ghraib prison.

This pattern continues to the present with the horrendous atrocities of the U.S.-directed Contras [revolutionaries] against the Nicaraguan people in the 1980s and the U.S. military "advisers" and CIA agents supporting the El Salvadoran torturers of their own population during the 1980s, which left 80,000 dead, disappeared or tortured to death. The U.S. invasion of Panama in 1989 was a military invasion of a highly populated urban area to arrest one person: Manuel Noriega. It left the neighborhood destroyed and close to 1,000 innocent Panamanians dead.

> *Terror and its corollary torture are absolutely essential to U.S. foreign policy.*

The U.S. army training of Latin American military [officers] at the School of the Americas in Fort Benning [Georgia], has produced dozens of horrible torturers and mass murderers, while the Army claims it teaches them "human rights."

Torture and the Purpose of Empires

It is important to realize that use of torture is not just for information. Its use is integral to the primary necessity of empire—to create terror in subject populations. The official line of the U.S. military is that torture does not work because the victim will say anything and the information is not "righteous." However, the torturers are experts in discerning what is "righteous" from what is not.

But that is not the main point. When the tortured just names the names of everyone he or she knows, this is valuable as well. The U.S.-supported dominators—in El Salvador, Guatemala, Chile and elsewhere—have routinely arrested, murdered or brutalized everyone named. The target is not just "subversives." It never has been. It is necessarily the general population—who are required to live in terror.

The purpose of empires is always economic. The purpose of the U.S. empire is that the poor and wretched of the world should accept U.S.-owned sweatshops paying starvation wages and U.S. corporations extracting the resources and wealth from their pliant countries while they remain in poverty and misery. Without terror, people would never accept the brutal conditions of death, deprivation, misery, hunger and disease that most of the people in the "grand area" endure for their entire lives.

If their rights were respected—political rights and human rights—then they would organize and defeat the empire at will. They would take steps to use the resources of their countries to benefit their own people. This is exactly what empire cannot allow. Only terror keeps them accepting the horror of their present lives. Terror and its corollary torture are absolutely essential to U.S. foreign policy.

9

The Abu Ghraib Prisoner Abuse Qualifies as Torture

The Medical Foundation for the Care of Victims of Torture

The Medical Foundation for the Care of Victims of Torture was founded in 1985 by members of Amnesty International. Over the past twenty years, it has organized volunteer medical professionals to provide medical treatment and psychological counseling to more than thirty-five thousand victims of torture worldwide.

In the spring of 2004, it came to light that U.S. soldiers had abused inmates at Abu Ghraib prison in Iraq. The prisoner abuse at Abu Ghraib—which included beatings, threats, the use of attack dogs, painful contortion, and sexual abuse—is physically harmful enough to be considered torture. Ever since the terrorist attacks of September 11, 2001, the U.S. government has been willing to use physical coercion as a tool to make suspected terrorists talk. Torture can only be prevented in the future if the U.S. government is willing to end its aggressive interrogation tactics and permit more international supervision.

The Medical Foundation for the Care of Victims of Torture is appalled by the treatment meted out by US military personnel to some of their prisoners in Iraq. One question the Medical Foundation has been asked a number of times since the furor broke is: 'When does mistreatment become torture?'

From the evidence examined by six US congressional committees, the Medical Foundation can state unequivocally that what took place in Abu Ghraib prison in Baghdad under US forces amounted to torture, which by agreed international definition, includes suffering which can be mental as well as physical.

> **❝** *The Medical Foundation can state unequivocally that what took place in Abu Ghraib prison in Baghdad under US forces amounted to torture.* **❞**

The "sadistic, blatant and wanton criminal abuses" listed by Major General Antonio Taguba following his investigation into the 800th Military Police Brigade at Abu Ghraib featured several methods employed by [Iraqi dictator] Saddam [Hussein's] torturers.

They included the punching, slapping and kicking of detainees, threats of execution, the use of dogs to terrorise, forcing prisoners to stand in contorted positions and the sodomising of a male prisoner with an inanimate object. Where Americans forced detainees to wear hoods, Saddam's torturers insisted that their victims were blindfolded.

One client of the Medical Foundation, who spent five years in Abu Ghraib under Saddam, says: "In all that time, I never saw the face of the men who tortured me. There was a hook outside each cell with five or six blindfolds on it. When you were taken away to be tortured, you were told to pick one as you left the cell."

He, like a number of the 3,322 Iraqi torture victims helped by the Medical Foundation since it first opened its doors in 1986, found recent images from Abu Ghraib brought back strong memories of the ordeal he endured.

Systematic Nature of the Torture

The Medical Foundation believes that far from being isolated incidents, the treatment of Iraqi prisoners by American service personnel reflected a systematic readiness to use torture, or other forms of cruel, inhuman or degrading treatment—which is also illegal under international law—to get results, or to intimidate or humiliate the captives.

Ever since the terror attack on the [World Trade Center] on September 11, 2001, the Medical Foundation has watched with growing alarm the growth of a lobby in America preaching physical coercion, and twice sought, unsuccessfully, a meeting with the US Ambassador to Britain to raise its concerns.

The existence of such a lobby was first made public in *The Washington Post* on 21st October 2001 when it was reported that some disgruntled FBI agents wanted to use physical force to obtain information from al-Qaeda suspects who were refusing to talk.

The Medical Foundation wrote immediately to the US ambassador seeking an assurance that no agency of the United States government would sanction the use of torture or other forms of ill-treatment in interrogating terrorist suspects.

We pointed out that evidence extracted under torture was not admissible in a US court and could therefore jeopardise the prosecution case against an accused.

> *The treatment of Iraqi prisoners by American service personnel reflected a systematic readiness to use torture . . . to get results, or to intimidate or humiliate the captives.*

We said that the use of torture would mean the US forfeiting its leadership role in all international and multilateral [forums] where human rights are discussed, and its bilateral relations with governments would no longer be based on respect for the rule of law.

We added that evidence shows that torture produces false or distorted information, while the State Department's reports to Congress on human rights abuses around the world provide incontrovertible evidence of how torture, once justified, eats at the fibre of many countries' law enforcement agencies and of the social contract itself.

And we also pointed out that several UN declarations and treaties to which the US as a signatory explicitly prohibit torture and cruel, inhuman or degrading treatment or punishment. Indeed, the US Constitution itself prohibits "cruel and unusual punishment."

A reply from an embassy official did not fully answer those concerns and a further letter was sent to the ambassador asking for an unambiguous public assurance that torture and ill-treatment would not be used. It was not forthcoming.

> *Several UN declarations and treaties to which the US is a signatory explicitly prohibit torture and cruel, inhuman, or degrading treatment or punishment. Indeed, the U.S. Constitution itself prohibits 'cruel and unusual punishment.'*

Instead, over the ensuing period, various pundits have stepped forward to suggest that non-lethal torture is acceptable. One Harvard Law School professor even suggested that courts should be allowed to issue warrants permitting torture, which in the Medical Foundation's view would implicate and corrupt the judiciary.

Such methods used by the US military have included sleep deprivation, noise bombardment, and forcing prisoners to stand in contorted positions for long periods of time.

"After 9/11 the Gloves Came Off"

Further evidence of the systematic nature of this abuse is that by the autumn of 2002 these so-called "stress and duress" techniques were in use in [the 2001–2002] Afghanistan [war] at the Bagram air base. *The Washington Post* brought them to world attention on 26th December 2002, and later the US military admitted that two detainees who died in December 2002 at Bagram were "homicide" cases under investigation.

The current Senate Armed Services Committee hearings in the US have focussed on this issue of the systematic nature of the abuses. Whereas President [George W.] Bush said that a few bad apples were responsible and would be brought to justice, the International Committee of the Red Cross [ICRC] called the abuses "systematic." General Taguba in his appearance before the Senate did not contradict his Commander in Chief, but he did indicate a need for further investigation to find out whether the practice had been systematic.

Given the attempted justifications for "torture lite" from October 2001 onwards, and the introduction of the techniques into interrogation at Bagram air base in 2002, followed by the transfer of the head of interrogation at [the US military prison in] Guantánamo Bay [Cuba], (General Geoffrey Miller) to Iraq in August 2003, with a new protocol for intelligence gathering at Abu Ghraib prison, it would appear that the practices were indeed systematic. The fact that some 50–70 interrogation techniques were in play in Iraq, according to the US military command, and that many of them have a sophisticated psychological element to them, including techniques of sexual humiliation adapted to the local cultural context, it is difficult to avoid the conclusion that the ICRC was correct to identify the procedures as "systematic".

Until now, precise details of the torture have been difficult to come by. In 2002 Cofer Black, former head of the CIA's counter-intelligence centre, told a Joint House/Senate Intelligence Committee hearing into the attack on the World Trade Centre: "That is classified information. Let's just say this: there was before 9/11 and there is after 9/11. After 9/11 the gloves came off.". . .

> *The system of abuse can be stopped, but not by evading the central question of its systematization. Apologies are not enough.*

Such interrogation techniques are certainly contrary to the [international] Geneva Conventions [governing treatment of war prisoners], and if found to be perpetrated on a large scale, or as part of a plan or policy, would fall within the remit of the International Criminal Court (ICC).

The ICC is a court of last resort, which means it can only come into play if the perpetrators are from a state which refuses to take action itself. It remains to be seen, however, if the international community is satisfied with the US response to the perpetrators in its military. If the response is deemed insufficient, then theoretically, any state that has ratified the statute could arrest US servicemen or women in their jurisdiction who are accused of being perpetrators and surrender them to the ICC.

The US has not ratified the ICC Statute, and has signed bilateral treaties with a number of signatory countries to avoid just that eventuality. They have also enshrined in law a statute that allows them to invade any country that, unlawfully in its view, is holding US service personnel. So theoretically, any move by the ICC to detain American servicemen or women suspected of human rights abuses could lead to a US invasion of Holland, where the court is based.

Can This System of Abuse Be Stopped?

The system of abuse can be stopped, but not by evading the central question of its systematisation. Apologies are not enough. Even prosecutions, though welcome, are insufficient to stop systematic abuse. Some of the techniques have been banned by the US, but only in Iraq. If they deserve to be banned in Iraq, surely they deserve to be banned worldwide.

A number of other aspects of detention and interrogation at Abu Ghraib (and elsewhere in Iraq, Afghanistan and at Guantánamo Bay) should be abandoned. There should be limits to incommunicado detention; detainees should have access to independent legal counsel and to members of their families on a regular basis. There should be no secret detention and no "rendering" of prisoners to other countries where torture by proxy can be implemented outside US jurisdiction.

No confessions or other information obtained by torture or ill-treatment should be invoked in legal proceedings—which is the reason that the Fifth Amendment to the US Constitution protects the individual from being forced to testify against himself. Such practices encourage the use of torture to obtain information and confessions.

Most important, there must be an improved prison regime that allows independent monitors to visit detainees on a more frequent basis. The ICRC has already visited all the prisons in question in Iraq, Afghanistan and Guantánamo Bay, but that alone has not stopped the abuses. The US Administration must agree to allow greater access to their inspectors and, in consultation with the ICRC, to publish the results of those visits.

10

The Abu Ghraib Prisoner Abuse Does Not Qualify as Torture

Ilana Freedman

Ilana Freedman is managing partner of the counterterrorism consulting firm Gerard Group International, and a deputy sheriff of Bristol County, Massachusetts. She has written numerous articles on terrorism and public policy.

The abuse of Iraqi prisoners by U.S. soldiers at Abu Ghraib prison is mild when compared to the torture that took place under the rule of former Iraqi dictator Saddam Hussein. When the two situations are treated as if they were on the same moral plane, it demonstrates how little the American public knows about how oppressive regimes overseas conduct themselves. The Abu Ghraib prisoner abuse—however desperate it may have been, and however much it might have violated international principles—does not qualify as torture. The prisoners were not killed or maimed, and the information they provided may very well have saved human lives.

Editor's Note: This viewpoint was written shortly after the incidents described were revealed to the public. Several months later, information became available regarding the prisoner abuse that was far more severe than what the author described, and would, under the author's own definition, constitute physical torture. The purpose of this article was to discuss the use of the term and not to support the use of "torture" as it is used to cause pain, injury, and death. At this writing, the complete facts are still under investigation.

The CIA has released a four minute videotape showing the torture at Abu Ghraib prison in Iraq. The press was invited to view this tape. It was considered an important insight into a very serious finding. Five people showed up. Only four actually watched the film in its entirety, and they probably wish they hadn't.

> // When you deal with an enemy who expects torture, mere conversation or interrogation is not likely to be enough to elicit the necessary responses in time to save the lives of others. //

This is not a video of prisoners being forced to assume humiliating positions, with their heads covered and their bodies naked, while in the custody of the United States military. This was a video of torture under the reign of [former Iraqi dictator] Saddam Hussein. It is a video of prisoners being beheaded, having their fingers chopped off one by one, and their tongues cut out with a razor blade. This four minute video tape, whose sound track is pierced by the horrible screams of Saddam's victims, is the stuff that a lifetime of nightmares are made of.

It is also a video that most of us will never see. No network or cable station will air it. It is too gruesome, too cruel, too sickening. Unlike the genre of grisly horror movies that draw so much box office attention, this film shows real people being tortured by men who love their jobs. What makes it so horrifying is that it is real. And because the media seems to have no interest, most of us will never begin to understand what real torture looks like.

The Context of Abu Ghraib

It will therefore be relatively easy for us to continue to say, as our own Sen. Edward Kennedy said on May 10, 2003, "Shamefully, we now learn that Saddam's torture chambers reopened under new management—U.S. management." Or as Massachusetts Congressman Marty T. Meehan said after viewing the photos from Abu Ghraib, he said, "There's no doubt in my mind that the abuses at Abu Ghraib constitute torture."

Not even close, gentlemen. Statements like these demonstrate the complete disconnect from which many in America suffer, a lack of understanding about the realities of war and the essential nature of cultures other than our own. We have been largely protected from the ugliness and cruelty that is a fundamental reality in other parts of the world.

When compared, for example, to the video-taped beheading of [U.S. citizen] Nick Berg [at the hands of Iraqi terrorists] or to the mutilations of the bodies of dead soldiers and contractors (which also were not shown on television), the excesses of our troops seem tame. And being frightened by a snarling dog doesn't compare to Saddam's use of hungry Doberman Pinschers to tear apart his helpless victims. When compared to this, the behavior of our soldiers in Abu Ghraib seems hardly worth mentioning.

> *What our soldiers did to their prisoners was not torture. It was mistreatment. . . . But in case we have forgotten, we are at war in Iraq.*

But, of course, we do mention it, as we should. We Americans like to think that we should take the high road in our commerce with the world. I do not disagree. If we are to continue to lead a world where in many places democracy is still a distant dream, we need to lead not by force but by example. Over the last 230 years we have done so—most of the time with great success. What took place at Abu Ghraib under our watch was offensive and reprehensible, but it must be taken in context and put into perspective.

The Challenge Soldiers Face

Almost everyone who has ever faced the business end of an enemy weapon or met the horror of terrorism face to face, understands that under conditions of battlefield stress, when the lives of comrades are at risk, there is little you will not do to keep them safe.

When you deal with an enemy who expects torture, mere conversation or interrogation is not likely to be enough to elicit the necessary responses in time to save the lives of others. Sleep deprivation, the withholding of food, the public humiliation of prisoners, have all been used by most intelligence services around the world for many years. They are all against the [international] Geneva Conventions [regulating treatment of war prisoners], and because we are obligated to abide by those agreements, our soldiers in the field sometimes face difficult, no-win choices.

The fact remains that what our soldiers did to their prisoners was not torture. It was mistreatment, it was assuredly unkind, and almost certainly uncomfortable and humiliating. But in case we have forgotten, we are at war in Iraq. The lives of our own sons and daughters, our husbands and wives, are at risk every day and may depend on the information that our intelligence receives from those whom they capture.

One thing we tend to forget is that the men imprisoned in Abu Ghraib were not Eagle Scouts. Some were terrorists, who would not hesitate to commit hideous atrocities on our own soldiers, were the situations reversed. Others were accomplices or supporters of those who were killing American soldiers and civilian contractors. Of course, they did not enjoy being humiliated. But the treatment they received at the hands of our soldiers didn't kill or maim, and it may have saved lives.

When the lives of our personnel are at stake, when time is of the essence, when hours or even minutes may make the difference between life and death, we should depend on our soldiers' ability and training to behave with honor, but also to do what is necessary to avoid putting others at risk in the name of political correctness.

If we wish to set a higher standard, as we should, but still need to obtain the intelligence necessary to protect our mission, we must be creative in finding methods that will break down the walls of resistance while still honoring the rules of war. Developing technology will help. Common sense and good training will also help. But it would be useful as well to stop the self-flagellation and public humiliation of our leaders and remember that we are at war and that we still carry the world standard for humanity and civility, even on the battleground.

11

The Abu Ghraib Prisoner Abuse Was Committed by a Few Disobedient Soldiers

Tammy Bruce

Tammy Bruce served for seven years as president of the Los Angeles chapter of the National Organization for Women. She is author of The New Thought Police: Inside the Left's Assault on Free Speech and Free Minds *(2001) and* The Death of Right and Wrong: Exposing the Left's Assault on Our Culture and Values *(2004), and is a regular guest on Fox News Channel.*

The abuse and humiliation of prisoners by U.S. soldiers at Abu Ghraib prison was inappropriate, but did not constitute torture. It was instead a reflection of our society's emphasis on pornography and sexual degradation as reflected in the lives of those accused of perpetrating this abuse. These people have a clear history of immoral conduct, including adultery and alleged domestic abuse. The abuse at Abu Ghraib should not reflect on the majority of soldiers, whose example of patriotism, discipline, and moral courage flies in the face of the torturers' shallow, artificial, and narcissistic worldview.

I was struck by how shocked members of the Senate were upon viewing additional pictures of the undisciplined, unprincipled freaks masquerading as members of our military at Abu Ghraib prison.

Tammy Bruce, "Why Abu Ghraib Matters," *Front Page Magazine*, May 24, 2004. Copyright © 2004 by the Center for the Study of Popular Culture. Reproduced by permission.

Keep in mind, according to reports from the Senators themselves, most of the additional pictures were of our soldiers having sex with each other—male soldiers having sex with female soldiers, that is.

Senators such as [Dianne] Feinstein [D-CA] and [Ben Nighthorse] Campbell [R-CO] expressed absolute shock at the pictures they saw. I'm shocked at how out-of-touch our Senators seem to be when it comes to the nature of what happened at Abu Ghraib.

> **❝** *I consider the vast majority of what happened at Abu Ghraib to be hazing—nothing more, nothing less.* **❞**

Now don't get me wrong—I believe when it comes to Al-Qaida leadership and operatives, anything goes. I don't care if you put women's underwear on their heads, or frankly, even pull out a few fingernails of those responsible for mass murder, to unmask their continuing plans for the genocide of civilized peoples.

It's called "torture lite," it works, and I'm all for whatever it takes to get information, and yes, to punish and annihilate terrorist leadership around the world.

The Worst in Ourselves

That said—I consider the vast majority of what happened at Abu Ghraib to be hazing—nothing more, nothing less. For weeks, all of us have been shouted at by the liberal media about how awful the events were, how having a man stripped naked in front of a woman was "torture," how making a prisoner wear women's underwear was "horrific," and the most recent "charge" of forcing men to wear maxi-pads.

Ah, the horror of it all! I hear that the next stage of the abuse is to make the Iraqis read *Ms. Magazine*. Heck, that would be torture for anyone! Combine that with forcing them to watch Lifetime Television (the Network-of-Horrible-Things-Are-Going-to-Happen-to-You-Because-You're-a-Woman) and I'm sure we'd have the location of [terrorist leader Osama] bin Laden in an hour.

From what I could glean from our shocked, just shocked Senators, it seems as though they have never realized that the pornography industry is one of the biggest industries in the world; that we have raised now two generations of men (and women) with graphic, obscene images which have made degrading behavior "sexy," "normal" and "exciting."

For the Senators who do not know, or have not cared to think about it, the growing scourge of pornography relies on the degradation and humiliation of women, the usual subject involved. What a perfect tool to implement in war!

And, dear Senators, how dare you be so shocked and surprised that those who appear to have been the most depraved, the most abusive, seem to have been as obsessed about recording not only the sexual humiliation of their victims, but to participate in it and wallowing in their own sexual subjugation as well.

Through modern culture each of us is being conditioned to accept, promote and reward the worst in ourselves. The amazing and hopeful news in all of this is that most Americans still reject this plan of Leftists [liberals] in control of social view of ourselves.

Violence and Depravity

Film, television and even radio have gone further and further into a pit of mindless violence, loveless sex and degrading discussion. Finally, we're demanding the FCC [Federal Communications Commission] do something about it, but that won't erase the decades of increasing depravity throughout all mediums of entertainment.

> *// What Democracy and freedom brings is the rule of law—not perfection, but a way to deal with the imperfect, and even the depraved, among us. //*

It is worth remembering, we are the greatest nation on Earth specifically because acts which are tantamount to hazing are surprising, and unacceptable, to most people.

In our efforts to maintain our perspective here, yes, we have promised Democracy to the people of Iraq. What Democracy and freedom brings is the rule of law—not perfection, but a way to deal with the imperfect, and even the depraved, among us.

As of this writing, Army Sgt. Charles A. Graner, Jr.,[1] one of the soldiers court martialed, seems to have defined his defense. His lawyer appeared on one of the many news programs [during the spring of 2004] and explained that Sgt. Graner was ordered to do the things he did by a superior, someone he could only identify as "Big Steve." Who Big Steve was he did not know. And oddly, neither does Sgt. Graner.

> *Nihilism and moral relativism has its grip on so many, and yet . . . so few in the military display the immorality the Left feeds on.*

This from a man, as *USA Today* reported, who has at least three protective orders granted against him by the courts at the request of an ex-wife who in court documents alleges Graner doing everything to her ranging from physical violence to videotaping her surreptitiously.

Sounds like something the Abu Ghraib prisoners are familiar with. With that background, it shouldn't be so surprising that soldiers charged have claimed Graner was the ringleader of the abuse. And as most of us now know, Lynddie England, the most prominently pictured woman involved, is Graner's "girlfriend" and pregnant with his child.

Of course, the blame game has started with a vengeance. No one, absolutely no one in this morbid game is willing to take responsibility for what has happened. That is, except for [U.S. defense secretary] Donald Rumsfeld and [President] George W. Bush, neither of whom have anything to do with the absurdity of the situation, but two decent men who are trying to do the right thing.

A Failure of Personal Responsibility

Instead, all those involved on the ground, ranging from Brig. General Karpinski, to PFC England, insist it was someone else,

1. Graner was eventually convicted and sentenced to ten years in prison.

some other person. We have "Big Steve." I'm sure at some point we'll also get the surprise appearance of the Abominable Snowman shouting orders at people, or the Grinch, or the Cat in the Hat, or perhaps it's been [pornographer] Larry Flynt.

In addition to the scourge of pornography, the lack of personal responsibility at first seems mind-boggling, but is not so surprising. We have all been inundated with a Leftist culture that drills into us that judgment is verboten; that standards of behavior are oppressive; that expecting more from people is racist, sexist or homophobic.

The Left has been obsessed with creating a culture that tells people nothing that happens to them is their fault. We see this reinforced all the time within our Injustice System.

I detail in my book *The Death of Right and Wrong*, judges and juries freeing murderers because they're "victims of a racist society" or fighting against the oppressor. Women who murder their children are set free because they are victims of "the cult of motherhood."

Nihilism and moral relativism has its grip on so many, and yet the good news is, the extraordinary news is, that so few in the military display the immorality the Left feeds on.

By counterpoint, the real story of Abu Ghraib is that our military, in its greatness and commitment to free people around the world, instills in 99.9 percent of its men and women in uniform the maturity, discipline and love of country which seems to help erase the depraved elements the Left has drilled into our young people now for decades.

We can choose to focus on the few who represent the worst, or we can remember that ours is a military that will not only save the world from itself and the Islamist-Fascists who dream of death and destruction. We can remember it is an American institution which creates "greatest generations," not by accident, but by training, principles, love of country, and for most, love of God.

12

The Abu Ghraib Prisoner Abuse Was Authorized by High-Ranking Government Officials

Eric Boehlert

Eric Boehlert is a senior writer for Salon.com. *He also writes frequently on public policy issues for other publications.*

The abuse of Iraqi prisoners by U.S. soldiers at Abu Ghraib prison in Iraq cannot be blamed solely on the alleged torturers themselves. The abusers could be the indirect result of orders from Brigadier General Janis Karpinski, who oversaw the use of military police to transform Abu Ghraib prison into an intelligence-gathering detention facility. The abuses could also be the more direct result of orders from civilian officials such as Undersecretary of Defense Stephen Cambone and Secretary of Defense Donald Rumsfeld, who favored the use of physical coercion as a means of information gathering. But the widespread abuse of detainees in Afghanistan, Cuba, and Iraq indicates that more than a few lone soldiers are responsible.

[In May 2004] as the Bush administration struggled to contain the Abu Ghraib prison torture scandal, Peter Feaver, a Duke University professor and former National Security Coun-

Eric Boehlert, "How High Does It Go?" *Salon.com*, May 28, 2004. Copyright © 2004 by Salon Media Group. Reproduced by permission of *Salon.com* at www.salon magazine.com. An online version remains in the Salon archives.

cil staff member, suggested a worst-case scenario for the White House: If "a senior civilian, or maybe even [Secretary of Defense Donald] Rumsfeld, [had] signed a memo that indicated, yes, sexual humiliation for prisoners is OK."

[Journalist] Seymour Hersh summoned that worst-case scenario to life with an article in the May 24 [2004] issue of the *New Yorker*, providing evidence alleging that Rumsfeld secretly approved a plan to use harsh interrogation methods on prisoners in Iraq—including methods that "encouraged physical coercion and sexual humiliation of Iraqi prisoners." The Pentagon labeled the article "outlandish, conspiratorial and filled with error and anonymous conjecture," but it did not specify the errors and had the sound of a classic nondenial denial. Rumsfeld's attempt to dismiss the piece did not forestall bipartisan calls in Congress for further investigation, with Sen. Carl Levin, D-Mich., the ranking member of the Armed Services Committee, declaring that Hersh's article raises the scandal to "a whole new level."

At the same time, *Newsweek* [reported] that in the wake of 9/11, White House counsel Alberto Gonzales advised President [George W.] Bush that the Geneva Convention articles that deal with interrogating prisoners of war might not apply to the war on terrorism. *Newsweek*'s revelation suggests that Gonzales memo may have established a foundation for the torture that followed.

> **"** *The more that is exposed, the more the Abu Ghraib scandal looks less like a case of renegade soldiers.* **"**

For weeks the Pentagon has suggested that the prison abuse cases arose from too little oversight at Abu Ghraib. That was clearly the finding of Maj. Gen. Antonio Taguba, who investigated the abuse allegations for the Army. But what if the opposite were true and those overseeing Abu Ghraib initiated the unlawful treatment? The more that is exposed, the more the Abu Ghraib scandal looks less like a case of renegade soldiers. How high up the chain of command does it go?

"That's the question—was the abuse a result of the absences of command guidance or the result of command guidance?"

says John Pike, an intelligence expert and the director of Global Security.org.

> *The idea was to turn the detention center into an intelligence-gathering outfit and, contrary to longtime Army regulations, make M.P.'s [military police] an integral part of the interrogation process to 'soften up' the prisoners.*

"You can busy yourself going through the military chain of command and looking at the actions of the [Abu Ghraib] guards," says Rep. Ellen Tauscher, D-Calif., a member of the House Armed Services Committee, who thinks the scandal's focus should be on top civilian leaders. "But the truth is, they were taking orders and the orders came from the Pentagon, which has complete and unfettered control of the war effort. There was a change in policy [at the prison]. Something caused people to vary from what was right and to 'amp it up,' and this is what you get."

A Secret Intelligence-Gathering Program

For Tauscher, the scandal is a case of déjà vu. In 2002 and 2003, during the feverish run-up to war with Iraq, the civilian leadership at the Pentagon, frustrated with the analysis it was receiving from the CIA about the level of threat posed by [Iraqi dictator] Saddam Hussein, took the extraordinary step of setting up a secretive, in-house intelligence shop staffed by handpicked hawks [prowar officials], to help maneuver stories that Iraq was an imminent "weapons of mass destruction"–level threat around the normal intelligence-vetting process. That effort was a success in providing the impetus that the Bush administration used to drive the country into war, but those stories have since been revealed as disinformation, much of it originating with neoconservative favorite Ahmed Chalabi, the [proposed] Iraqi [prime minister] who boasted about being a "hero in error."

Fast-forward to the summer of 2003. Frustrated with the lack of good intelligence about the absent WMDs and the simmering internal Iraqi resistance, the civilian leadership at the

Pentagon reportedly took the extraordinary step of allowing Iraq's largest prison, Abu Ghraib, to be put under the command of military intelligence instead of the military police. The idea was to turn the detention center into an intelligence-gathering outfit and, contrary to longtime Army regulations, make M.P.'s [military police] an integral part of the interrogation process to "soften up" the prisoners.

"Do you see a pattern?" asks Tauscher, who raised concerns last year about the administration's top-down pressure to produce a certain kind of war intelligence. It was the same type of pressure that led Lt. Gen. Ricardo Sanchez, who oversees the U.S. fighting force in Iraq, to hand over authority of Abu Ghraib [in November 2002] to the 205th Military Intelligence Brigade. Then Maj. Gen. Geoffrey Miller, who at the time was running Camp X-Ray at Guantánamo Bay, where prisoners are detained indefinitely as unlawful "enemy combatants" outside the Geneva Convention gave orders to "Gitmo-ize" [that is, make it more like Guantánamo Bay, Cuba] the prison.

"Miller was sent to turn Abu Ghraib into an intelligence production center rather than a detention facility, and that's where the Geneva Convention stuff starts to get in the way of winning the war," Pike says. The obvious differences between the two prisons—X-Ray holds those thought to have ties to al-Qaida—seem to have been overlooked in an effort to uncover better intelligence. The International Red Cross, in fact, has reported that 70 to 90 percent of the prisoners at Abu Ghraib have been imprisoned there by mistake, simply rounded up in dragnets.

> *The International Red Cross . . . has reported that 70 to 90 percent of the prisoners at Abu Ghraib have been imprisoned there by mistake, simply rounded up in dragnets.*

"The White House was frustrated by the lack of information being obtained from detainees and was screaming for intelligence about WMDs and insurgent leaders," says Vince Cannistraro, a former CIA counterterrorism chief. "Commanders were under pressure from Washington, and that translated into taking off the gloves."

Who Is Responsible?

One key to the debate about who bears ultimate responsibility centers on the mystery of authority at Abu Ghraib. If it's true that a group of rogue M.P.'s ran wild inside the prison, then the chain of command would likely go up to Brig. Gen. Janice Karpinski, who was in charge of all the prison operations in Iraq, and the scandal would essentially remain contained within the Army.

But if military intelligence officers, perhaps acting according to Rumsfeld's secret orders, are to blame for the abuses, or if last November [2003] fateful decision to amp up the intelligence-gathering efforts is a significant factor in the debacle, then the spotlight will likely bypass Karpinski and her M.P.'s and start climbing up the chain of command.

> *The part played by the private contractors at Abu Ghraib remains a mystery, as does their possible punishment.*

"If it's military intelligence and you go up the chain of command, you get to the Pentagon and to [Stephen] Cambone and Rumsfeld," explains Cannistraro. In Cambone's testimony before Congress the undersecretary of defense for intelligence contradicted Taguba's assertion that military intelligence had control of Abu Ghraib. Cambone's version, which evoked skepticism from some members of the Senate Armed Services Committee, was that military intelligence was acting as a sort of building supervisor, taking care of the prison grounds while the M.P.'s maintained control of the prisoners.

"Cambone is trying to create a firewall around the top chain of command," says Greg Thielmann, who ran military assessments at the State Department's Bureau of Intelligence and Research until he retired last October. "If guards were following military intelligence and [ranking M.I. officer] Col. Thomas Pappas, then who was he reporting to? Ultimately you get to Cambone—and that firewall is not going to hold. One way or another, these guys above the identified culprits [running the prison] are in big trouble."

"I think it will go to Cambone," says retired U.S. Army Col. David Hackworth. "The original game plan was to fry a few fish: sergeants and corporals. Then they decided [they'd] have to fry some bigger fish: Pappas and Karpinksi. That won't work because they'll blow the whistle [on] Cambone, who's the ultimate boss of intelligence and a micromanager."

> *At some point . . . the scandal will reach a decisive moment and either halt at the low-ranking M.P.'s or go up the chain.*

Cambone does not deny that last summer he encouraged Miller and a team of 30 specialists to travel to Abu Ghraib in hopes of improving the prison's intelligence gathering. But Cambone testified that Miller was not sent to Iraq with official directives, that he himself did not encourage M.P.'s to become involved in interrogation and that when Miller subsequently recommended breaking down the wall between military intelligence and the M.P.'s at Abu Ghraib, he never briefed Cambone about it. (Cambone also told senators that he did not read the Taguba report and was unaware of the abuse photos until after CBS's "60 Minutes II" broke the story about prison abuse on April 28 [2004].)

Sen. Hillary Clinton, D-N.Y., spelled out the potential trouble for Rumsfeld and the White House: "I, for one, don't believe I yet have adequate information from Mr. Cambone in the Defense Department as to exactly what Gen. Miller's orders were, [and] what kind of reports came back up the chain of command as to how he carried out those orders."

Sen. Jack Reed, D-R.I., was equally skeptical of Cambone's testimony: "Gen. Miller suggested that guard forces be used to set the conditions [at Abu Ghraib]. Yet you did not choose to ask about this. You were completely oblivious.". . .

Prosecuting the Abusers

The debate at the center of the legal jockeying is about who controlled Abu Ghraib—military intelligence or the military police. According to the statement he gave to investigators last January, Army Reservist Jeremy Sivits, who struck a plea-bargain agreement with the government and has agreed to testify against his fellow soldiers, acts of random violence were perpetrated on prisoners. He insists they did not come down as orders from above but were carried out by low-ranking personnel like Spc. Charles Graner, who reportedly punched prisoners unconscious, hit wounded detainees with baseball bats, and posed for photographs atop a pile of detainees.

But last week, Graner's attorney pointed a finger at military intelligence officers and private contractors as the ones who barked orders to M.P.'s, who were simply following those orders. Graner's attorney suggested that Sivits is implicating low-ranking soldiers as part of his plea agreement.

The part played by the private contractors at Abu Ghraib remains a mystery, as does their possible punishment. Under the Uniform Code of Military Justice, "persons serving with or accompanying an armed force in the field" are subject to the code "in time of war." That might cover the contractors, whose actions captured in photographs clearly violated the code. However, the U.S. Court of Appeals for the Armed Forces previously held that the military lacked jurisdiction over civilian employees of the Armed Forces during the Vietnam War because, the court ruled, the phrase "in time of war" contained in the code meant a war formally declared by Congress. The Vietnam War was never formally declared by Congress. Nor was the invasion of Iraq.

The unfolding investigations could take two parallel tracks. At some point . . . the scandal will reach a decisive moment and either halt at the low-ranking M.P.'s or go up the chain. . .

The administration cannot find support inside the military, either. "For military officers, this scandal is outrageously infuriating; it has tarnished everybody," says Ralph Peters, a retired Army intelligence officer and regular contributor to the reliably conservative *New York Post* editorial page. "The civilian side at the Pentagon, like Cambone—they were the ones trying to cover this up, not the military. I believe Donald Rumsfeld needs to go because he has lost the trust and respect of the officer corps."

13

The U.S. News Media Overrated the Significance of the Abu Ghraib Prisoner Abuse

Oliver North

Oliver North is a former aide to the U.S. national security adviser.

The U.S. news media are always willing to cover events that portray the United States in a negative light, but are extremely reluctant to report on atrocities committed against Americans. The abuse at Abu Ghraib, though reprehensible, pales when compared to murder and mutilation of four U.S. security contractors and the decapitation of U.S. civilian Nicholas Berg, which occurred at roughly the same time as the alleged abuse but generated a fraction of the media publicity. The U.S. media interest is politically motivated; by consistently describing the United States as an oppressor rather than a victim, the U.S. media can criticize political administrations with which their members disagree.

Americans are so good at self-flagellation that even a heinous act by others may be insufficient to remind us that we're not so bad after all. [During the spring of 2004] the media has bludgeoned the Bush Administration, the Secretary of Defense and the U.S. military for the mistreatment of detainees in Iraq's Abu Ghraib prison.

Oliver North, "Where Are Media When Jihadists Torture and Murder Americans?" www.humaneventsonline.com, May 14, 2004. Copyright © 2004 by Human Events, Inc. Reproduced by permission.

Now we have the horrific, videotaped murder of an American civilian, 26-year-old Nick Berg. The perpetrators of this ghastly act [Iraqi terrorists] proudly shout "Allahu Akbar" (God is great), over the screams of the young man as they hack through the sinews of his neck and then proudly display his severed head for the camera. The tape concludes with a prepared statement by one of the executioners claiming "the dignity of the Muslim men and women in Abu Ghraib and others is not redeemed except by blood and souls."

As shocking as this video is—and it is truly revolting in a way that churns your gut—it is nothing new. Radical Islamic jihadists [that is, Muslims who believe they are fighting a holy war] have been perpetrating this kind of horror against Americans for more than 20 years. And, as if to substantiate the jihadists' claims that it's not their fault, the "blame America first" crowd in the U.S. media looks for ways to point out how we really deserve what we're getting. Equally consistent, the Arab press parrots ours in ways that incite more violence while "leaders" in [theocratic] Islamic states remain mute—or worse, condone—the atrocities.

When Americans Are Targeted

On March 16, 1984, CIA Station Chief William Buckley was abducted and then tortured to death in a Beirut [Lebanon] dungeon. I carried the agonizing photographs and tape recordings of his brutal beatings back to CIA Director William J. Casey. No Islamic leaders condemned the kidnapping and murder. The U.S. media rationalized his treatment as the consequence of being a CIA employee.

> *Radical Islamic jihadists have been perpetrating . . . horror against Americans for 20 years . . . [while] the 'blame America first' crowd in the U.S. media looks for ways to point out how we really deserve what we're getting.*

On May 28, 1985, David Jacobsen, the administrator of the American University Hospital in Beirut, where most of the people treated were Muslims, was taken hostage on his way to work. No Islamic leaders denounced the perpetrators. After Jacobsen's release in November 1986, his 18 months of torture were ignored by a U.S. media more intent on castigating the Reagan Administration for an "arms for hostages deal" than in punishing his captors. The same situation applied for all the other Beirut hostages.

> **"** *Since only a small handful of people were involved [in Abu Ghraib], we all naively assumed that this would be a one or two-day story. . . . We were wrong.* **"**

On February 17, 1988, Marine Col. William Higgins was kidnapped and subsequently murdered in Lebanon. Though the United Nations filed a complaint that one of their observers had been "taken," Islamic leaders were again unheard. When Colonel Higgins' remains were finally recovered in 1991, the silence of the U.S. media was deafening.

By 21 February 2002, when *Wall Street Journal* reporter Daniel Pearl was butchered in Pakistan, the jihadists had moved to a new level. Photographs and audiotapes were deemed inadequate to depict the horror they intended to show us—and their adherents. Daniel Pearl's murderers held him for a week—while they plotted his brutal murder—in front of a video camera. And while Islamic leaders were once again mute—this time the U.S. media responded to the horror. Danny Pearl was, after all, one of their own. The European press seized on this aspect of the atrocity and decried the heinous act as "an attack on freedom of the press." That Daniel Pearl was a Jewish American was hardly mentioned.

The Selective Silence of the U.S. Media

On 31 March [2004], just prior to my third trip to Iraq, four American civilians, escorting a shipment of humanitarian food and medicine were ambushed, shot, mutilated and dragged through the streets of Fallujah [Iraq] before their bodies were burned and hung from a bridge over the Euphrates [River]. When I arrived in the city days later, I was informed that the perpetrators had taken pains to notify members of the Arab press prior to the grisly event. The U.S. media pointed out that the security contractors should have known better than to drive through a city where the U.S. was so highly resented. No Islamic leader rose to condemn the atrocity.

Days later, on 15 April jihadists in Iraq released the video-taped murder of Fabrizio Quattrocchi, a 36-year old Italian. Though the press praised the courage of the young security guard facing certain death by proclaiming, "Now I'm going to show you how an Italian dies," members of the Euro-media immediately called for the withdrawal of "foreign troops from Iraq" and the resignation of Italian Prime Minister Silvio Berlusconi. It was a one or two-day story in the U.S. media. From Ramadi, Iraq, I looked in vain for any Islamic leader who would rise to denounce the assassins or condemn the killing.

I was in Fallujah when the story broke about the abuses at Abu Ghraib. The soldiers and Marines I was with agreed that while the actions described were inexcusable, this was "old news" because it was about activity that had occurred months before. Since only a small handful of people were involved, we all naively assumed that this would be a one or two-day story. The events, and those engaged in them, had all been investigated. Those responsible had been, or were in the process of being, punished or prosecuted. There was no cover up. The military had already begun to rectify the command and organizational deficiencies that led to the abuses. We were wrong. We sadly underestimated the effect of such a story in a political year.

Because of the twisted, sado-sexual nature of the photographs taken at Abu Ghraib, the prison abuse story is deemed to be more "newsworthy" than a long litany of jihadist atrocities. The silence of the sheiks, mullahs and imams [Islamic religious leaders] isn't worthy of newsprint. No broadcast minutes will be wasted on commentaries complaining about the lack of opprobrium from "moderate" Islamic leaders. The vivid horror of Nick Berg's bloody severed head is insufficient to usurp the "prison abuse" story from the headlines. The U.S. media smells blood—not of murdered Americans—but of [U.S. defense secretary] Donald Rumsfeld. Never underestimate our penchant for self-flagellation.

Organizations to Contact

The editors have compiled the following list of organizations concerned with the issues debated in this book. The descriptions are derived from materials provided by the organizations. All have publications or information available for interested readers. The list was compiled on the date of publication of the present volume; the information provided here may change. Be aware that many organizations take several weeks or longer to respond to inquiries, so allow as much time as possible.

American Civil Liberties Union (ACLU)
125 Broad St., 18th Fl., New York, NY 10004-2400
(888) 567-ACLU
e-mail: aclu@aclu.org • Web site: www.aclu.org

Founded in 1920, the ACLU is a national organization that works to defend civil liberties in the United States. It publishes various materials on the Bill of Rights, including regular in-depth reports, the triannual newsletter *Civil Liberties*, and a set of handbooks on individual rights.

American Enterprise Institute (AEI)
1150 Seventeenth St. NW, Washington, DC 20036
(202) 862-5800 • fax: (202) 862-7177
Web site: www.aei.org

The AEI favors conservative public policy, particularly a strong national defense that is largely free of international regulation. It publishes numerous books and policy papers, an annual report, a monthly newsletter, and the *American Enterprise*, a popular bimonthly magazine.

Amnesty International (AI)
322 Eighth Ave., New York, NY 10001
(212) 807-8400 • fax: (212) 463-9193
e-mail: admin-us@aiusa.org • Web site: www.amnesty.org

Made up of over 1.8 million members in over 150 countries, AI is dedicated to promoting human rights worldwide. Since its inception in 1961, the organization has focused much of its effort on the eradication of torture. AI maintains an extremely active news Web site, distributes a large annual report on the state of human rights in every country on Earth (as well as numerous special reports on specific human rights issues), and publishes the *Wire*, the monthly magazine of AI.

Association for the Prevention of Torture (APT)
Route de Ferney 10, Case Postale 2267, 1211 Geneva 2, Switzerland
+41-22-919-2170 • fax: +41-22-919-2180
e-mail: apt@apt.ch • Web site: www.apt.ch

Hosted in Geneva, Switzerland, the APT actively works to end torture worldwide. It publishes the *APT Newsletter* three times per year, maintains a detailed annual report on torture around the world, and prints specific manuals and special reports detailing specific issues and events pertaining to torture.

European Committee for the Prevention of Torture and Inhuman or Degrading Treatment or Punishment (CPT)
Human Rights Building
Council of Europe, F-67075 Strasbourg Cedex, France
+33-3-8841-3939 • fax: +33-3-8841-2772
e-mail: cptdoc@coe.int • Web site: www.cpt.coe.int

The CPT originated with the 1987 passage of the European Convention for the Prevention of Torture and Inhuman or Degrading Treatment or Punishment, an international treaty ratified by forty-five members of the European Council. The CPT performs site visits in participating countries to ensure that no torture or other inhuman treatment is taking place. It maintains a large online database detailing torture reports and site visits and publishes numerous reports, standards, and reference documents pertaining to torture.

Human Rights Watch (HRW)
350 Fifth Ave., 34th Fl., New York, NY 10118-3299
(212) 290-4700 • fax: (212) 736-1300
e-mail: hrwnyc@hrw.org • Web site: www.hrw.org

In 1988 several large regional organizations dedicated to promoting human rights merged to form HRW, a global watchdog group. HRW publishes numerous books, policy papers, and special reports (including a comprehensive annual report), sponsors an annual film festival on human rights issues, and files lawsuits on behalf of those whose rights are violated.

International Committee of the Red Cross (ICRC)
Washington, DC, Regional Delegation
2100 Pennsylvania Ave. NW, Suite 545, Washington, DC 20037
(202) 293-9430 • fax: (202) 293-9431
e-mail: washington.was@icrc.org • Web site: www.icrc.org

Founded in 1863, the ICRC is one of the few organizations to have won the Nobel Peace Prize (and did so on three occasions: in 1917, 1944, and 1963). It was the ICRC that led to the creation of the Geneva Conventions on the treatment of prisoners of war, the wounded, and medical personnel, among others. Today the ICRC continues its mission by investigating reports of human rights violations, assisting in disaster relief, and working on behalf of those who are wounded or imprisoned in wartime.

The Iraq Foundation
1012 Fourteenth St. NW, Suite 1110, Washington, DC 20005
(202) 347-4662 • fax: (202) 347-7897
e-mail: iraq@iraqfoundation.org • Web site: www.iraqfoundation.org

Founded in 1991 by Iraqi expatriates, the Iraq Foundation is dedicated to promoting democracy and human rights in Iraq. It maintains an online news page, hosts seminars, and publishes numerous special reports.

U.S. Department of Justice (USDOJ)
950 Pennsylvania Ave. NW, Washington, DC 20530-0001
(202) 514-2000
e-mail: askdoj@usdoj.gov • Web site: www.usdoj.gov

The U.S. Department of Justice is responsible for enforcing U.S. federal laws and assisting local and international law enforcement efforts as needed. The official USDOJ Web site features numerous special reports, a "Kids' Page," and a frequently updated news site.

U.S. Department of State, Counterterrorism Office
PA/PL, Room 2206, 2201 C St. NW, Washington, DC 20520
(202) 647-6575
Web site: www.state.gov/s/ct

The U.S. Department of State's Counterterrorism Office is responsible for coordinating international efforts to fight terrorism. The office's Web site includes pages dealing with current events, patterns of global terrorism, homeland security, and other issues pertaining to counterterrorism efforts.

U.S. Naval Base at Guantánamo Bay, Cuba
PSC 1005, Box 25, FPO AE 09593

The U.S. Naval Base at Guantánamo Bay hosts hundreds of accused Taliban and al Qaeda fighters imprisoned during the Afghanistan War of 2001. Human rights groups argue that these detainees have been denied access to the U.S. criminal justice system and subjected to "stress and duress" interrogation techniques. In *Rasul v. Bush* (2004), the U.S. Supreme Court sided with the detainees and ruled that they have the right to challenge their status in U.S. civilian courts.

World Organisation Against Torture (OMCT)
Organisation Mondiale Contre la Torture International Secretariat
PO Box 21, 8 Rue du Vieux-Billard, CH-1211 Geneva 8, Switzerland
+41-22-809-4939 • fax: +41-22-809-4929
e-mail: omct@omct.org • Web site: www.omct.org

The OMCT is a global network of three hundred organizations dedicated to fighting torture and other forms of violence. It initiates numerous campaigns that assist victims of torture, promote the rights of children, monitor police activity, and take other measures designed to combat torture. OMCT maintains a large news archive and publishes many special reports on torture and violence.

Bibliography

Books

Amnesty International *Take a Step to Stamp Out Torture.* London: Amnesty International, 2000.

John Conroy *Unspeakable Acts, Ordinary People: The Dynamics of Torture.* New York: Alfred A. Knopf, 2000.

Alan M. Dershowitz *Why Terrorism Works: Understanding the Threat, Responding to the Challenge.* New Haven, CT: Yale University Press, 2003.

Bertil Duner *An End to Torture: Strategies for Its Eradication.* New York: St. Martin's, 1999.

Duncan Forrest, ed. *A Glimpse of Hell: Reports on Torture Worldwide.* New York: New York University Press, 1996.

Seymour M. Hersh *Chain of Command: The Road from 9/11 to Abu Ghraib.* New York: HarperCollins, 2004.

Brian Innes *The History of Torture.* New York: St. Martin's, 1998.

Sanford Levinson, ed. *Torture: A Collection.* New York: Oxford University Press, 2004.

Chris Mackey and Greg Miller *The Interrogators: Inside the Secret War Against al Qaeda.* New York: Little, Brown, 2004.

Daniel P. Mannix *The History of Torture.* Gloucestershire, UK: Sutton, 2003.

Michael Ratner and Ellen Ray *Guantanamo: What the World Should Know.* White River Junction, VT: Chelsea Green, 2004.

Periodicals

Martin Edwin Andersen "Is Torture an Option in the War on Terror?" *Insight on the News,* June 17, 2002.

Jed Babbin "Post-Saddam Crimes at Abu Ghraib," *National Review Online,* May 3, 2004.

John Barry, Michael Hirsh, and Michael Isikoff "The Roots of Torture," *Newsweek,* May 24, 2004.

Jonah Goldberg "Barbarians at the Geneva Gates," *National Review Online,* June 17, 2004.

John Gray "A Modest Proposal," *New Statesman,* February 17, 2003.

Harper's	"Out of Mind," May 2004.
Seymour M. Hersh	"Torture at Abu Ghraib," *New Yorker*, May 10, 2004.
Hendrik Hertzberg	"Terror and Torture," *New Yorker*, March 24, 2003.
Michael Hirsh, John Barry, and Daniel Klaidman	"A Tortured Debate," *Newsweek*, June 21, 2004.
Vincent Iacopino, Allen Keller, and Deborah Oksenberg	"Why Torture Must Not Be Sanctioned by the United States," *Western Journal of Medicine*, May 2002.
Danielle Knight	"Trade in the Tools of Torture," *U.S. News & World Report*, November 24, 2003.
Giovanni Maio	"History of Medical Involvement in Torture—Then and Now," *Lancet*, May 19, 2001.
Andrew C. McCarthy	"Torture: Thinking About the Unthinkable," *Commentary*, July/August 2004.
Johanna McGeary	"The Scandal's Growing Stain: Abuses by U.S. Soldiers in Iraq Shock the World and Roil the Bush Administration," *Time*, May 17, 2004.
Tom McGrath	"And Lead Us Not into Temptation," *U.S. Catholic*, November 2000.
Fida Mohammad et al.	"Understanding Torture and Torturers," *Journal of Evolutionary Psychology*, August 2002.
Karen Olsson	"The Torturers Next Door," *Mother Jones*, May/June 2003.
Stephen Pincock	"Exposing the Horror of Torture," *Lancet*, November 1, 2003.
Eyal Press	"In Torture We Trust?" *Nation*, March 31, 2003.
Amanda Ripley	"Redefining Torture," *Time*, June 21, 2004.
Amanda Ripley	"The Rules of Interrogation," *Time*, May 17, 2004.
Daniel Rothenberg	"'What We Have Seen Is Terrible': Public Presentational Torture and the Communicative Logic of State Terror," *Albany Law Review*, Winter 2003.
Meinrad Scherer-Emunds	"Zero Tolerance for Torture: An Interview with Sister Dianna Ortiz, O.S.U." *U.S. Catholic*, January 2004.
David Shapiro	"The Tortured, Not the Torturers, Are Ashamed," *Social Research*, Winter 2003.
Johan D. van der Vyver	"Torture as a Crime Under International Law," *Albany Law Review*, Winter 2003.
Claudia Wallis	"Why Did They Do It?" *Time*, May 17, 2004.

Index

Abu Ghraib prison
abuse of prisoners at, 12–13, 59
amounts to torture, 60
con, 66–68, 69
is result of Bush administration
policies, 74–76
con, 24, 72
media focuses on, 84
sexual nature of, pornography as
factor in, 71
was a result of wartime
conditions, 30
failure to prosecute murders at, 15
Geneva accords govern treatment
of detainees at, 27–28
Afghanistan, use of "stress and
duress" techniques in, 62
Alexander, Keith, 33
Amnesty International, 49

Begin, Menachem, 37
Berg, Nicholas, 29, 67, 81, 82
Black, Cofer, 49, 63
Boehlert, Eric, 74
Bowden, Mark, 39
Brennan, William J., 23
Bruce, Tammy, 10–11, 69
Buckley, William, 82
Bush, George W., 15, 56, 72
Bush administration
authorization of stress techniques
by, 13
denies Geneva protections to
Guantánamo detainees, 14, 26,
32–33
flouting of international law by,
33–34
hypocrisy and use of coercion by,
52–53

Cambodia, 56
Cambone, Stephen, 74, 78, 80
Campbell, Ben Nighthorse, 70
Cannistraro, Vince, 77, 78
Caplan, Lincoln, 31
Carter, Jimmy, 17–18
Central Intelligence Agency (CIA), 66
interventions in foreign
governments by, 56–57
Chalabi, Ahmed, 76
Chile, 56–57

Clark, Ramsey, 18
Clinton, Bill, 33
Clinton, Hillary, 79
Constitution, U.S. See Eighth
Amendment; Fifth Amendment
Cowan, Bill, 48
crucifixion, 9
cruel and unusual punishment, 9

Death of Right and Wrong, The
(Bruce), 73
Department of Defense (DOD)
maneuvered intelligence on Iraq,
76–77
stress matrix of, 13
Dershowitz, Alan M., 22, 50
due process clause, 24

Eighth Amendment, 9
enemy combatants, designation of
Guantánamo detainees as, 26
England, Lynddie, 72

Feaver, Peter, 74
Feinstein, Dianne, 70
Fifth Amendment, 22–23, 64
Freedman, Ilana, 65

Gachelin, Louis, 9, 18
Geneva Conventions, 11, 13, 26
background of, 32
dangers of making exceptions to,
31
denial of, to Guantánamo
detainees, 14
mutual respect as basis of, 26
provisions of, 28
reasons for denying protections of,
29–30
stress and duress techniques
violate, 63
con, 46–48
Gonzalez, Alberto, 32, 75
Graner, Charles A., Jr., 72, 80
Guantánamo detainees
denial of Geneva protections to, 14
is justified, 28–29
interrogation techniques used on,
35–36
use of torture on, 49–50
Guardian (newspaper), 10

Guatemala, 56

Hackworth, David, 78
Hammurabi, Code of, 9
Harman, Sabrina, 33
Hersh, Seymour, 75
Higgins, William, 83
Holzer, Henry Mark, 16
Human Rights Watch, 14, 49
Hussein, Saddam, 47

Indonesia, 56
International Committee of the Red
    Cross (ICRC), 62, 64, 77
International Criminal Court (ICC),
    33, 63–64
interrogation techniques. *See* stress
    and duress techniques
Iraq War
    Bush administration's rationale for,
    31
    vs. war on terrorism, 27–28
    Bush administration has treated
        as the same, 33
Israel, efforts to regulate use of
    torture in, 46
    problems with, 14
    in "ticking-bomb" situations, 50–52

Jacobsen, David, 82–83

Karpinski, Janice, 72, 78, 79
Kennedy, Edward, 66
Korea, 56
Koubi, Michael, 50, 51
Kyoto Protocol, 33

Landau, Moshe, 50
Landau Commission, 50
Laos, 56
Leon, Jean, 9, 18–20
Levin, Carl, 75

Malinowski, Tom, 35
Martin, Glen T., 54
McNamara, Robert, 56
media
    breaks story of Abu Ghraib abuses,
    79
    focuses on U.S. misbehavior, 82–84
Medical Foundation for the Care of
    Victims of Torture, The, 59
Meehan, Marty T., 66
Metzler, Jakob von, 50
military intelligence, Abu Ghraib
    abuses and, 77, 80
Miller, Geoffrey D., 15, 77, 79
Mohammed, Khalid Sheikh, 39

Montell, Jessica, 51–52
Muhammad, Shah, 49
Myers, Richard, 33

Newsweek (magazine), 75
New Yorker (magazine), 75
New York Post (newspaper), 80
Nicaragua, 57
Noriega, Manuel, 57
North, Oliver, 81

Pappas, Thomas, 78, 79
Pearl, Daniel, 29, 83
Peters, Ralph, 80
Pike, John, 75–76
pornography, led to Abu Ghraib
    abuses, 71
prisoners of war, Geneva
    Conventions on, 28

al Qaeda, 47
    is not covered by Geneva accords,
    28–29
Quattrocchi, Fabrizio, 84

Reed, Jack, 79
Roanoke Times (newspaper), 55
Roth, Kenneth, 11, 12
Rumsfeld, Donald, 33, 56, 72, 74
    Abu Ghraib abuses and, 78, 80
    on interrogation techniques at
        Guantánamo Bay, 35–36
    rescinds torture methods, 37

Sanchez, Ricardo, 77
self-incrimination
    ruling on, in Leon case, 20
    Supreme Court on torture and,
    22–23
September 11 attacks, 9
sexual humiliation, of Abu Ghraib
    prisoners, 12–13
    pornography as factor in, 71
al-Shibh, Ramzi bin, 48
"shock the conscience" test, 24
Sivits, Jeremy, 79
60 Minutes II (TV series), 79
*State Department Policy Planning Study
    No. 23* (1948), 55
stress and duress techniques, 10,
    36–37
    examples of, 46
    purpose of, 28
    use of, in Afghanistan, 62
    violate Geneva accords, 63
        con, 46–48
stress matrix, 13
Suharto, Mohamed, 56

Supreme Court, on torture and self-incrimination, 22–23

Taguba, Antonio, 60, 61
Taliban, loss of POW status by, 29
Tauscher, Ellen, 76, 77
Thielmann, Greg, 78
"ticking time bomb" scenario
  Israel's use of coercion in, 50–52
  torture may be justified in, 17–18, 22
Time (magazine), 47
torture
  abuse of Abu Ghraib prisoners constitutes, 60
  con, 66–68, 69
  vs. coercion, 52–53
  definitions of, 9, 29
  evidence extracted under, limitations on, 22–23, 61
  as integral to empires, 57–58
  may be justified in ticking time bomb cases, 17–18, 22
  post-9/11 lobby for, 61
  psychological vs. physical, 17
  regulation of, 24–25
    problems with, 14–15
  treaties prohibiting, 11
treaties, prohibiting torture, 11

truth serum, 23–24

UN Convention Against Torture, 11, 13
United States
  as empire, 54, 55
    use of torture is integral to, 57–58
  International Criminal Court and, 63–64
  interventions in foreign governments by, 56–57
  media focuses on misbehavior by, 82–84
USA Today (newspaper), 72
"use immunity," 23

Wall Street Journal (newspaper), 49, 83
war on terrorism
  Geneva Conventions and, 32–33
  torture as tactic in, 9–10
Washington Post (newspaper), 48, 61, 62
Washington Times (newspaper), 37

Yoo, John, 26

Zubaydah, Abu, 47, 48